LYNETTE JENNINGS

Meredith Books   Des Moines, Iowa

Lynette Jennings No Compromise Decorating
by Lynette Jennings
Editor: Paula Marshall
Executive Editor: Denise L. Caringer
Contributing Editor: Mindy Pantiel
Art Director: The Design Office of Jerry J. Rank
Copy Chief: Terri Fredrickson
Copy and Production Editor: Victoria Forlini
Book Production Managers: Pam Kvitne, Marjorie J. Schenkelberg, Rick von Holdt, Mark Weaver
Contributing Copy Editor: Ro Sila
Contributing Proofreaders: Sue Fetters, Sherry Hames, Erin McKay
Indexer: Elizabeth Parsons
Contributing Photographer: Emily Minton Redfield
Cover Photographer: John Haigwood, Haigwood Studios
Editorial Assistants: Kaye Chabot, Karen Mc Fadden
Editorial and Design Coordinator: Mary Lee Gavin

Meredith® Books
Editor in Chief: Linda Raglan Cunningham
Design Director: Matt Strelecki

Publisher: James D. Blume
Executive Director, Marketing: Jeffrey Myers
Executive Director, New Business Development: Todd M. Davis
Executive Director, Sales: Ken Zagor
Director, Operations: George A. Susral
Director, Production: Douglas M. Johnston
Business Director: Jim Leonard

Vice President and General Manager: Douglas J. Guendel

Better Homes and Gardens® Magazine
Editor in Chief: Karol DeWulf Nickell
Deputy Editor, Home Design: Oma Blaise Ford

Meredith Publishing Group
President, Publishing Group: Stephen M. Lacy
Vice President-Publishing Director: Bob Mate

Meredith Corporation
Chairman and Chief Executive Officer: William T. Kerr

In Memoriam: E. T. Meredith III (1933-2003)

All of us at Meredith® Books are dedicated to providing you with information and ideas
to enhance your home. We welcome your comments and suggestions. Write to us at: Meredith Books, Home Decorating
and Design Editorial Department, 1716 Locust St., Des Moines, IA 50309-3023.

If you would like to purchase any of our home decorating and design, cooking, crafts, gardening or
home improvement books, check wherever quality books are sold.
Or visit us at meredithbooks.com.

CONTENTS

MY JOURNEY HOME

"We look for safety, shelter, only to find the of memories, the of our

joy, and peace
answer is in a collection
foundation
present and future."

DEAR FRIEND,

What I have learned in all these years of making homes my livelihood and passion—building, designing, planning, furnishing, writing about, and filming them, and, of course, answering thousands of your questions—is that home isn't a place or a building. Home is a feeling in your soul. Your things form the scrapbook of your life. They deserve to be used and displayed to make your home beautiful, not just plopped into rooms, not arranged to suit some unrealistic "ideal" setting you saw in a magazine. Those are the compromises that erode personal style.

After all these years I have learned that home isn't a place or a building. Home is a feeling in your soul.

I've experienced the good fortune and the aggravation of renovating while living in several homes (some of my friends count 22!). I have learned that regardless of the stage of my life—some more challenging than others—my home has evolved and materialized into a group of loved things: A comfortable, never boring, memory-laced, mismatched collection to which I add and subtract.

My home has evolved and materialized into a group of loved things: A comfortable, never boring, memory-laced, mismatched collection to which I add and subtract.

Like the seasons change on a wonderful mature tree, my "home life" has blossomed into colors, faded into

My Atlanta house couldn't have been more different architecturally than my current western ranch. But both are my style because they offer comfort and peace.

neutrals, blossomed again, grown new style branches and dropped old ones, ever developing into an unplotted collections of me and my family. Ours is truly an individual style, not in an exotic sense or the reinvention of some period design, but an assembly that speaks of our blended lives. It has a certain confidence that comes from choices made with love, and not fear, and the strength of NO COMPROMISES. Oh, that's not to say there weren't at times great deliberation over certain chairs or china. But now when I look around me, I see my life in three dimensions, and not a designer's showplace. I see memories old and fresh, good times and bad. I see a marriage left behind, the crystal in my china cabinet, and a new one with three more children in my oversize dining table that serves a family of seven and their drop-in friends. I see financially impulsive times in my 7-foot-tall, 14th century gilt mirror, and I see hard-luck times in the $15 rocker.

Our home life is an assembly that speaks of blended lives. Choices made from love.

Even now as I write at my breakfast table, I sit in one of four maple chairs, the one still unfinished, a new page in my life's scrapbook, a reminder of my breast cancer diagnosis that postponed my staining project. I was fortunate to beat the disease, so maybe I'll leave it that way for awhile—a proud symbol of a battle won.

Our Toronto Victorian was an eclectic hodge podge of a blended family's collections of "stuff." Some precious and some just the paraphernalia of life. It all seemed to fit in a deconstructionist renovation where exposed brick walls married sophisticated Victorian moldings. Crazy, but that's us!

Yes, I've moved many times. A new envelope, new views, new geography, but my true home has been with me always like old slippers and new earrings. Even my two girls who were with me all the way through the interim 16 years of single momdom, never felt the changes–just new bedroom colors. Even now as 20-something adults, their own life-scrapbooks begun, they have become collectors of comfort—each in their own style. One is city chic and the other colorful country. My college-aged stepchildren are developing their own "scrapbooks" even as they make their bedspread choices for

To say the process of decorating one's home is part of life's journey seems a bit overly profound. But, in a way, it is.

campus apartments. Of all the things I hoped to share with them, I believe that one is the courage to make those choices and to avoid compromising their style.

To say the process of decorating one's home is part of life's journey seems a bit overly profound. But, in a way, it is. What's inside those walls and how you live with those choices, the relative importance you give things by their placement, reflects the who, when, and where you are in your life's journey. No matter if we live on a farm or in the city or in a soccer-mom-suburb, wherever we lay our heads at night, that is our home, our retreat, our place where we are who we are, for better or worse, no matter what others may think—NO COMPROMISES.

Totally casual and "undecorated" is our style at the ranch. It's an anything-goes kind of place. Stone walls 2-foot-thick, embossed concrete floors with old (not antique) rugs. Kick off your shoes and snuggle in amidst the craft and art I've collected over the years. (And yes, that's my guitar!)

"Our home has always been

a collection of memories."

This loved mirror looks tiny on our western wood walls! The salvaged French candle chandelier made it from Toronto's dining room and the chairs are slipcovered in washable canvas. One loved mirror, it goes with so many different home styles. This is a mirror that was purchased many, many years ago. What worked in our Atlanta living room with such overwhelming impact, some years later, works with a more diminutive impact in our dining room of our home today. Personal "Love" items that transcend time and place.

Always celebrate the connection of your home to your life.

Your home is a celebration of you and your family, everything about your history, your memories and daydreams, your coming together as partners, your children, and their children. Antique or modern, every time you make choices, be guided by what they add to your life: Table tops that wear like a family diary, every mark a story. Chairs that beg to be tipped in laughter. Candles that remind you of the smells of long ago Christmases. Cushy sofas long enough for Autumn Sunday naps. A hall mirror that one day might reflect your daughter or grandaughter's veiled image on her wedding day. Always celebrate the connection of your home to your life; don't apologize for it, and don't compromise.

Home isn't a look, it's a feeling. A place where memories are made and legacies are formed. That said, why would we for one second hesitate to make choices based on anything but what our heart desires? Why would we even for an inkling be distracted by a new product display, a neighbor's comment, or a "dream home" featured on TV or in a magazine other than for the inspiration it provides?

Call it conviction, stubbornness, determination. To eliminate the pressure. The fear of decision. To dig for the courage to live how and with what makes us happy. That's decorating without compromise.

Come with me. Let's go home. *Lynette Jennings*

Unfinished timber, stone, and pot-bellied stoves—a big change from our Toronto Victorian and the Atlanta 1960s glass box, but it's still us, because we focus on warmth and a relaxing environment. Different dog? Yes, Golden Retriever, Cruise, went to doggie heaven. Meet Whiskey, our Aussie.

I've always wanted to try a true furnished kitchen. An assemblage of antique and reproduction cabinets and farm tables instead of contemporary built-ins give this ranch kitchen its flavor. Practical? Absolutely. And you can't beat the atmosphere.

"I've found my heart in the kaleidoscope colors of Western slick rock, my power in the endless turquoise sky. This is now my home."

Some snapshots of my ranch home. CLOCKWISE FROM TOP LEFT: My new "rose garden" is prickly pear cactus; Here come the guest bedrooms, much to the chagrin of the cattle—Oh, excuse me; did we disturb you?; My daughter and I check out our new "backyard;" My new wardrobe; it's chic and practical; A childhood sleigh finds a new home; I'm creating my shrine to the single mom who homesteaded our land in the early 1800s; Yes, I made these stockings—the first Christmas at Dirty Boot Ranch; This wagon was an impulse buy; got to have it!

DECORATING FOR LIFE

ASK YOURSELF THESE QUESTIONS: *Do I love my home now? Does my house reflect my family? Am I proud of my style? Does my home feel warm and secure?*

If you answered "No" to any of these questions, you've made compromises. For reasons usually related to budget, time, and stage of life, it happens; but we can fix it. Decorating isn't about picking colors and arranging furniture. It's about making a house comfortable and secure, a nurturing environment that allows you

If any room doesn't feel right or comfortable, it's a sure bet you've made compromises in the decor.

to be you. The place to love, to relax, to recharge, to embrace life. So the most important goal in decorating is to create a home that makes you *feel* good!

Decorating is an *interpretation* of everything you want your home to be and to feel like. Colors, furniture, accessories, and collections are the pieces that form the giant quilt of dreams and memories to snuggle into. We're going to work on this step-by-step throughout this book. Your home should make you smile. If it doesn't, it's bad karma. That sounds a bit over the top, but I really feel it's all connected. It's not really that complicated. It simply has to do with "stuff." Think of it this way: If,

Decorating is simply an interpretation of everything you want your home to be.

when you get up every morning, the first things you see are a childhood dresser that you never liked, second-time-around curtains, and a "what was I thinking" sofa, your day is attitudinally compromised!

This delightful room is a patchwork quilt of color, pattern, furniture styles, and loved travel memories. It's no particular academic decorating style. It's what I call the epitome of personal style.

Some people will say that these are minor details in the larger, nobler scheme of life. Yes and no. Whether you are right-brain oriented or left, you are emotionally and psychologically affected by what appears in your visual bubble. Negative visuals—things you don't like, even get aggravated about—have an effect on your attitude and, subsequently, your life. Everything in your line of sight, which means everything in your home, has the potential to create a positive, pleasurable, uplifting effect on your psyche or to have a negative, irritating impact. Even when you've lived with something negative for so long it seems invisible, I believe it still haunts your subconscious with niggling little pricks of dissatisfaction. Take a quick mental inventory of your house. Red flag those negative items. Later I'll show you how to edit them out.

There are things in your house you would never part with. You LOVE them for all kinds of reasons: comfort, color, memories that evoke feelings of elation, pride, even affection. These are keepers. And then there are items that are there for all the wrong reasons: a living room full of furniture bought just because it all matches, or a hurriedly purchased family room set that you know isn't you at all. Sometimes, even when a room looks coordinated, you may not be happy with it. It makes you feel as though you're living in someone else's house or a showroom; it doesn't feel right. Why? COMPROMISE. You've made decisions for the sake of style or color, but didn't consider how the end result made you *feel*.

Decorate using items and colors that evoke pleasant thoughts or good memories.

If you love it, use it. You'll find that your taste, what your eye sees as beauty, has a self-coordinating effect—once you edit out the things you never liked to begin with!

"Start by identifying your

Living in an apartment doesn't give you permission to compromise! Build an atmosphere with your personal loves. Ignore the walls. If landlord white bugs you, integrate white as a color in your scheme and not just a neutral background.

loves.”

In most cases when I work with a client I find the decorating solutions lie in a tangle of existing furniture and accessories, not in new schemes. Together, we sort and prioritize, rearrange, and recolor according to what they *love* and what will add emotional value to their lives. In most cases, the stuff of life is already there. But the clutter created by continuous COMPROMISES has created confusion. Halfway through the process, I see the light in their eyes as I get close to what they were trying to achieve. *"Yes, that's it...that's what I wanted...wow, let's go. I can do this now!"*

The process of decorating starts with taking an honest look at *who you are*. That's what good design professionals do: get to know you and your family as intimately as is practical before they make any suggestions. Later I'll give you an exercise that will help *you* get to know *you* better.

Then you need THE PLAN. Its foundation is based on your gut reaction to your home and only the things that are important to you. Most people accumulate things without a PLAN, with choices driven by need. You need a new sofa, so you head out on a Saturday. Before you pick up the cleaning and drop the kids at soccer, you decide on a fabric that's immediately available (because you don't want to wait 16 weeks for a special order). The fabric sort of coordinates with the carpet that came with the house, even though you hate the carpet. Three days later, you take delivery

Make decorating choices based on how items make you feel.

What did you do on your summer vacation? — no essay required! Decorate while you shop for souvenirs. Forget the "I was here" T-shirts and go for the market lady's hand-dyed batik scarf that is soon to be a living room pillow. Exotic accessories, like the ones here, always tend to be naturally dyed, deep rich earthy colors. They're wonderful art pieces. Most importantly, you love them and the memories.

of a sofa you don't *love,* or feel just neutral about it. COMPROMISE. Eventually, you're surrounded by things that were "the only one available," "on sale," "free from the in-laws," "needed before Christmas," or were chosen because "it's the latest thing." COMPROMISES all.

Then you try to integrate the latest purchase into what you already have, frustration turns to panic, and you start trying quick fixes: buying another piece of

A chain reaction of compromises is the basis of most decorating problems.

furniture or a rug you don't really like but kind of fits in. You leave the walls off-white in hopes that the neutrality will somehow unite this disparate collection. After all, off-white goes with everything, right? WRONG! I see this all the time and it breaks my heart. You're so close, but you've lost your center, your focus. You've made a string of choices disregarding your emotional connection to your home and furnishings.

But hidden in with the COMPROMISES are the items chosen for the right reason: You LOVE them! Yes, yes, yes! Hang on to this thought!

Black magic. A table, three chairs, and a cabinet originally covered in dull brown stain were transformed with a primer and five coats of black acrylic paint. New white leather upholstery was not a big investment for these chairs. Now you can afford a show-stopping oversize chandelier. Decorating on a budget is all about trade-offs. And keep this in mind: You simply cannot make a mistake with black and white.

WHY WE COMPROMISE

THE GRASS ISN'T GREENER, IT'S JUST BEEN ART DIRECTED. One evening, as you tuck into your end of the sofa, you take a good look at the family room. You don't like it. Dullsville. The bookshelf that never got built has become an aggravation instead of a fun project. The corner is naked and the books are in boxes. And the carpet you were going to replace when you moved in is still there. The sofa looks tired even though it's only two years old. And the windows are still covered with the privacy roll-up blinds bought the evening you moved in. Then it happens. "Enough...*let's do something about this house*!" And off you go.

On your next grocery run you find yourself in the magazine aisle browsing decorating titles. Dozens of glossy, high-color covers: "50 Ways to Decorate a Bathroom," "Thirty Ways to Color Your Kitchen," and "16 Gorgeous Dream Rooms." All find their way into your cart. After dinner, you flip your way through spread after glossy, propped, and professionally lit spread of idealized homes. You look up dreamily from your reading and...that's the end of it. You fold the laundry and make lunches for tomorrow, all the while thinking, "How on earth could I transform this mixed-up collection of stuff of mine into something that beautiful without throwing everything out and starting over?" Fantasizing over a magazine home, if you don't mind my saying so, is about as realistic as

Forget perfection and consider comfort in every choice. Ask yourself: Is this a room for real life?

Comfort is the No. 1 priority. You know how it takes a while to get comfortable with new things? So don't go shopping for the latest trend. Instead browse thrift shops, garage sales, and family attics for items with personality and worn edges. Picture this room without the floral cushions and shabby window frame—among other, clearly not-new things. Then think about what you would put in a bare-bones room.

coveting the shape of *Vogue*'s lanky, airbrushed cover model!

The home you want is not the one in a magazine. Every life is unique and that results in every home being unique. If you look closely at some of those magazine photographs, you'll find a mismatched conglomeration of things just like yours. They've just been art directed: $500 worth of fresh flowers, a truckful of lights to cast that perfect 3 p.m. glow across the fireplace, $300 worth of styled baked goods casually propped on the kitchen counter suggesting a life of leisurely mornings spent perfecting puff pastry. And then there is the art director who crops anything "imperfect" out of the photo. Come on, I can do that to your house too! Comparing your home to these isn't fair.

Look closely at some of those magazine shots, and you'll find a mismatched conglomeration of things just like yours!

The value of those magazine homes is inspiration. Look at the photos for ideas. Look at the relationships between furnishings, colors, and light. The way a certain rug color complements a maple floor in a photograph may inspire a paint color behind your maple armoire. You see? NO COMPROMISE: Gather ideas only to *enhance*, and not replace, what you already have and love.

The only rooms you'll be happy with are the ones you create yourself, not copies of stylized rooms.

Be patient. A room full of personality like this one wasn't accumulated in a single shopping trip. Perhaps a plain coffee table sat in the middle until one day that chunky, pine trunk just jumped into view, and home it came. Or maybe it sat in the attic for years until someone suddenly realized how perfect it would be in the family room. You can't plan for that—but you can be open to it happening.

TRENDS ARE FOR TEA TOWELS

When you shop to coordinate new items with what you already have, do you go home empty-handed, frustrated that you are hopelessly out of style? Maddening, isn't it?

When trends intimidate you, belittling your personal style, then I say *STOP*. When you find yourself measuring your taste against what the media and retailers say you must have, well...I want to stick my head out the window and, inspired by that wonderful scene in the movie, *Network,* shout, *"I am not going to take this anymore!"*

Trends stimulate those who are *developing* a style. Trying to update what you have and love with trends that are typically short-lived and extreme most often creates even more confusion. But, to your advantage, eventually the trends cycle around to a look that's pretty close to what you want. So wait. Like a carousel of exotic foods, you must be confident in your taste and search for a look that matches your sensibilities.

The art, architecture, interior design, and fashion industries create trends as a way of reinventing themselves. They explore new material technologies, pushing the style envelope. It's stimulating and curious. We can't deny the highest form of artistic development any more than we should curtail science just because we don't understand it. Progress deserves respect. But to be intimidated by high design is akin to a crafter becoming disillusioned with her

Trends eventually cycle around to a look that's close to what you have.

Let's play Musical Chairs! All of these chairs are now design classics, readily available and pretty mainstream. But initially, each chair was a bit radical, at least one step out of the ordinary at the time. We have the daring and the trendsetting to thank. Keep an eye on what they're doing, but don't follow just to follow; be selective in adopting any trendy style. Only if you love it, do it.

evening's project because it doesn't live up to gallery standards.

There are those who can afford to invest in leading-edge style. The advancement of our artistic culture depends on their sophistication and commitment. Theirs are often the homes you see in magazines.

Your reality is likely different. You're working with a limited number of puzzle pieces that you have to put together in a pleasing manner. Your home is a collage of

Think of your home as a collage of things you love, arranged comfortably, not as a trendy magazine photo.

loved items, arranged for comfort. What's especially nice is that the arrangement needn't be permanent. You have the freedom to move your "stuff" any way you care to, any time. The high-design home is a ballet of pieces selected for specific spaces, and things rarely move. I've had a lot of experience with those houses and, frankly, they bother me; move one item and the whole works crumbles. I've met homeowners

terrified to move anything because their designer put it there. When they have a party, their designer has to supervise. Whoa, that's very scary. That's not what you want. So loosen up. You probably have more flare than you give yourself credit for.

NO COMPROMISE: Be confident. Choose trends only when they reflect your personal style.

Loosen up. The "before" snapshot is a perfect example of packaged-room blues. When you buy the pieces as a batch, you're likely to group them in a pretty standard formation. By simply swapping out the chairs, it's easier to visualize a more relaxed, comfortable furniture grouping and to build on that casual approach. The process starts with the confidence to NOT do the expected!

THE STATUS THING

Are you afraid of what someone else is thinking about your choices? Okay, now we have to talk about a bigger life issue here. Status is a tough one: We don't readily admit that it matters; we know it shouldn't. But it does. Why?

Women are nesters. We fix, fuss, and arrange our worldly possessions to make a pretty, comfortable place to live. We've done this since our days in caves. Pots were arranged, mud walls decorated with herb and mineral paints, designs woven into baskets and stitched into clothing. Pride of home has always existed. The more precious the goods, the higher your position in the tribe. The cave was the original status symbol.

Over time, decorating a home has turned into an anxiety-inducing exercise in seeking approval.

So since the beginning of time homes have represented position within the community. A cultural evolution that has pressured the joy, artistry, and personal caring out of nesting. Now decorating has become a paralyzing, frustrating, esteem-shattering process of designing our homes for the approval of others. Confidence buster! Have we forgotten the truest meaning of *home*?

NO COMPROMISE: Your home is the one place where you should be comfortable, safe, and free to live your way. You should be proud of it. Let everyone envy your courage!

Will "they" think you're crazy? Red walls to match a red rug? Most would shy away from this combination: "Too much red!" Not so here. An equal balance of red and off-white. Take your courage from the examples you see in this book. While the furniture may not be your style, look closely at combinations that might apply to your own collection. If you love red, use it—lots of it!

"Decorate with your things

That's personalizing. "

Raid your cedar chest, your garage, your crafts room, and keepsake boxes. Decorate with your own special things without editing them

for fashion. It's incredible how what you might consider a humble item, given center stage on a mantel, takes on the status of fashion.

But that's not even the real point. An item's value to you, the attached memories, is what's important.

A BEAUTIFUL HOME IS NOT ABOUT MONEY

A big budget doesn't solve problems; rather it has the potential to magnify them. I've found the best homes, the happy homes, are those with moderate budgets and lots of personal expression. More than money, decorating takes guts. It's harder to trust your instincts than to be swayed by exterior influences. You have to be stubborn, patient, and demanding of the marketplace. Don't buy what you aren't passionate about. NO COMPROMISE: Invest in yourself and your vision of how you want to live.

ARE YOU AFRAID TO MAKE A MISTAKE? You're just plain scared. Well, I can appreciate that. But what exactly is a mistake, anyway? Who is the judge? I've seen people and even professional designers do some of the wildest, and sometimes, most awful things to a room. But are they mistakes, or are they simply not my taste? "The eye of the beholder" is probably one of the most profound phrases in art and design. It's your house. If you like something do it or at least try it to see if you do like living with it.

Are you afraid of what someone else thinks of your home? Whoa! Let's stop and talk here. Status shouldn't matter, but it does. Why? Pride of home.

The media-driven pressure to be perfect, live perfectly, serve the perfect dinner, and have perfect children has made us prisoners, and that makes me angry. Perfection is an impossible goal, impractical and unlivable. Besides, who is determining the standard? I don't know about you, but I've had enough! *I'm* even feeling the pressure. I can only

No window dressing. Slipcovers and a well-worn table. Wicker rescued from a curbside. Nothing expensive here, but this room is loaded with style and elegance. That is the power of No Compromise!

imagine the case of "willies" you must have. I want to be free to try things and fail, to love what others may not like, and to have confidence to live in my own skin, my style—in fashion or not.

For years, I have been asked by fans—swatches and photographs in hand—to give them a decorating answer. What

Your home is the one place where you should be free to live your way. Let everyone envy your courage!

color? What flooring? What window treatment? Where to put the sofa? Without exception, I turn the question around and ask: What would *you* like to do? I'm not going to give you the answer.

"Well, I'm not sure. I'm scared of making a mistake. I'm afraid I won't like it after it's done. I'll feel stupid."

Just think about this: Nothing is a mistake if you really like and want to do whatever it is. So what's your answer?

"Well, I really love blue; I've loved blue since I was little. My husband says it's up to me, but he likes blue too."

So why are you asking me? DO IT.

The reason you ask is to be assured that you can do what you really want, and it will be OK. Well, I'm telling you now. IT'S OK.

Nothing is a mistake if you really like it.

NO COMPROMISE: *Decorating is all about you*—not me— *and your home.*

Take the flop test. Your mother would gasp at this suggestion: When no one is looking, rate your living room by taking the "flop down, snuggle in, and tuck your bare toes under the cushions" test. Too formal for such a thing or did you love it? This room tells me to slouch and snuggle in with my dog. Who cares if I live in Kansas—I love the ocean. That's my style.

"Your kitchen can be your

living room. Why not?"

No-rules decorating. We live in our kitchens. We eat, cook, pay bills, do homework, chat, read, plan, dream... so let's make it truly us! It is really the "living" room, so decorate accordingly. Use your art, upholstery, and wood furniture instead of cabinetry.

DON'T KNOW HOW TO START?

Try two things to jump-start the decorating process: Move the furniture. It's harmless, and you can always move it back. And paint a wall. What's a can of paint? If you don't like it, you can always paint it back. It's the least expensive thing you can do to change the look of a room. Even if you paint it back the original color you've learned something. Simply put, three coats of paint cannot equal failure.

Maybe you've lost your objectivity. I often get excited about some space that the homeowner doesn't see as wonderful. So often homeowners are sure their house is featureless, their furniture is ugly, and they have no clear style. Every time, I see something they don't. We'll work with most of what they have, wrapping it around their lifestyle. Happy home. Happy homeowner. NO COMPROMISE.

Every house has at least one redeeming, even exciting, feature. Find it and play it up.

Boring bookshelves or your favorite feature? Play it up if you love it. When you have a fabulous collection like these whiteware molds to display, built-ins are wonderful. But if you have a den full of shelves and your collections are small—make a collection. On this gorgeous woodwork rows of river rocks would be enchanting. Remember, it's how you display that makes the ordinary interesting. Against a plain background, unusual shapes become art.

GET READY FOR AN ADVENTURE!

Now you're ready to start a process that will guide you in not only improving your home, but potentially your life! It feels that good: It's not about starting over; it's about assessing how you want to live, then taking inventory of the architectural spaces, the furnishings, and accessories you most enjoy in your home. You see— all the answers to your decor dilemmas are rooted there. Out of that, you can create a plan, a "look" strategy, that will grow with you, and that you can modify as your life changes—all with confidence and without regret. But promise me as we work through this together—NO COMPROMISES!

All I can do is provide a path and offer advice; starting now, you're in control of decorating your home!

NOW THEN...ASK YOURSELF THESE QUESTIONS AGAIN:

Do I love my home now?

Does my house reflect my family?

Am I proud of my style?

Does my home feel warm and secure?

Then put yourself in the right frame of mind to change every "No" into a "Yes."

A pool table in the living room? Based on personal experience, I applaud this decision because I did it in one of my homes! That choice helped keep the family together all evening when the boys were teens. That's the beauty of No Compromise decorating—your home revolves around the way you live and everyone's comfort level is maximized. Why live any other way?

"Decorating. It's not about starting over, it's about assessing how you want to live, then taking inventory of the features and items you most enjoy and support your lifestyle."

What awkward corner? There's no such thing. Every nook, cranny, and alcove is an opportunity. Would you prefer a plain box? Much harder to make interesting and more expensive. Is it the table that makes this dormer interesting or are you drawn to the jar of flowers and napkin placed on the diagonal? For me, the table could be anything; the flowers and family photos make this sun-lit alcove special.

UNDERSTANDING YOUR SPACE, YOUR SELF

FOR MANY, DECORATING HAS BECOME AN OVERLY STRUCTURED FORMULA: Sofa under the window, chairs on either side of the fireplace, anchored with matching end tables and lamps. Then neutrals for walls and window coverings. And last, accessorizing in two steps: First put out the sentimental things. Second, fill the empty spaces with trendy things, rotated throughout the year, to inject just a touch of "in"-ness. Uh-oh. Trouble.

It takes objectivity and sensitivity to decorate your home. Opposites? No, complementary points of view.

Hey, this is your *home!* Where you live, hang out, where you meet life's challenges, where you show your love to those close to you, where you grow, learn, grieve, and sing. It deserves more attention and respect than that. Think of your home as the backdrop for your life's story.

Use your objectivity and sensitivity to decorate your home. Opposites? No, complementary points of view. *Be sensitive to your needs.* Be aware of where your frustrations are coming from. Just like the career coaches who tell us to take courage in our instincts about life choices, your relationship with your home requires that degree of sensitivity too. *You need objectivity* to look at what you have with fresh eyes. When we live with the *same* furniture and accessories, grouped the *same* way in the *same* rooms, even as we move from house to house, we lose the ability to see each piece creatively. So let's clear the canvas and create a new picture, still working with what you have.

Think of your home as the backdrop for your life's story.

Your favorite chair, the morning sun streaming over your shoulder...your favorite place in your imagination can be for real in your home. Find that window, then park your chair. Build the room around what's left! Notice here there is no sofa, just comfy chairs. No rules! Do it your way.

STEP 1

LEARN HOW YOUR HOUSE WANTS TO LIVE. The first step in decorating has little to do with furniture and accessories. It's about understanding the place where you live and how you relate to its shapes, traffic patterns, and views. It's amazing how many people I meet who, when asked to draw their floor plan indicating the placement of windows and doors, have to think really hard to identify even the basic shapes of rooms.

As you relearn your house, be sensitive to how *it* wants to live. Look for the flow and natural light. Pathways ("traffic patterns" in design lingo) suggest where furniture placement feels right. Block the direct line between the kitchen and the television with a sofa parked broadside, and you'll fight it every day. You can contrive against the architecture, but it will never feel natural.

As you relearn your house, be sensitive to how it wants to live. Look for the flow and sources of light.

NO COMPROMISE: Never make decisions for design's sake. *Your house has to live your everyday life. You and your house must work as a team.* Your house has potential, talent, and flexibility. You can make it work for you, but you have to listen to it first.

LET YOUR HOUSE SPEAK TO YOU. Decoration is deeply connected to architecture—plan, traffic patterns, views, and light. It's supposed to enhance and integrate the architecture and not be independent of it. Does this mean you absolutely must use only contemporary furniture with contemporary architecture and traditional furnishings with traditional architecture? No—of course you can mix it up. But then you are deliberately opposing

Tucked away. Everyone loves to get cozy, snuggle, cocoon at times. We're nesters, cave dwellers, male and female. That primal urge demonstrates itself when we need peace, love, rest. And so often we find it at one end of the sofa or another, the corner of the sectional, or in a bed shoved against the wall.

the character, an intriguing case of opposites attracting. This enhances the architecture by drawing attention to the dichotomy. This also causes artistic tension which is exciting, although not comfortable for everyone.

A California ranch is an open, relaxed one-story plan, with meandering rooms that flow together. Today's new homes with kitchens and great rooms that flow from the front foyer are much the same. Traditional furniture has a hard time in this environment because it wants tight groupings. A 50-50 mix of traditional and contemporary will loosen the stiffness.

On the other hand, floor plans that nest smaller rooms with doorway-to-hall connections, as in bungalows and Victorian cottages, invite more disciplined arrangements. Pattern and color schemes are easy to control under these circumstances, making each room a special event.

I have met people who have moved from a cottage-style home filled with cozy furniture into a new home with an open floor plan, and they are very uncomfortable. The furniture doesn't work. They wallpaper, trying to add the warmth of pattern and color, but are flummoxed when they can't find a defined start-and-stop point. So they resort to off-white. What a shame! Was this a good choice? When they bought the house, they were likely wooed by the light and open space. It can be impressive, and it looked like a good investment. But was it *really* right? Maybe what they really

If a room is uncomfortable ask yourself why. Does it feel too open or too closed in? That can be changed.

Long sight lines make little rooms big. One of my favorite tricks is to create long sight lines. I like to be able to see clear, uninterrupted floor for as far as possible. It tells me I can move fast, I can dance, I can spread my wings, I can see the sunlight clock the day on the hardwood floor.

"Bigger

is better in small rooms."

Bigger is better in small rooms! Don't be afraid of oversize furniture and bold patterns. If you want open space, take down a wall. If you want "cozy," tighten up the room. Space seating furniture away from walls with bookcases and tables. Build around the fireplace. Pull chairs up to the coffee table. This is the invitation to the living room you may be missing.

needed was a traditional home with *more rooms*, equaling the needed space, rather than an open concept that really amounts to just one big room.

When this situation is severe and my clients are very unhappy, I ask them to frame in those large openings, separating the rooms from each other, to effectively control the furniture arrangements and light. The effect is cocooning. After you rethink the relationship between you and your home, and if you come to realize the architecture isn't working with the decor, know that it's a challenge that can be resolved.

Go back to how you felt about your house when you saw it the first time. Let's work on recapturing the romance.

THE ROMANCE EXERCISE. The emotional connection with a house is most obvious when you experience the house empty, when you can see the scale of the rooms and the light, and clearly see the materials that clad the walls, floors, and ceilings. Go back to how you *felt* about the house when you saw it the first time. While the previous owner's decorating partially influenced your connection, there was something that drew you to this house over the alternatives. Remember that special hour between when their furniture moved out and yours moved in, and you saw the house with little more than paint, paper, and carpet. You knew at that moment where your favorite chair should be, and the view you wanted to see from your corner of the sofa...and then you placed everything in the same groupings in the same rooms with the same pictures and vases as it was in your previous house. Oh, the missed opportunities! Let's work on recapturing the romance.

Close up an open concept with a library divider. French doors, a solid wall, and wall units are all mini-architectural ways to section oversize rooms. In this case, a two-sided library dividing wall robs only 2 feet from the overall length of the room. As for atmosphere, think about old school library tables—solid and purposeful.

Understanding the physical plan is easy. Take the time to make a dimensioned floor plan. All it really takes is a tape measure, some graph paper and a pencil, and the commitment of an evening or two. Include every door and window. Use a compass to note the direction of the sun's patterns. As you draw the plan, imagine each room without furniture and color, naked.

MAKE A LIST OF WHAT YOU LOVED WHEN YOU BOUGHT THE HOUSE. Every house has positive and negative areas from an emotional standpoint. Areas that feel too small or too large, areas where the light sparkles at a certain time of day, depressingly dim spots, and nooks that store and crannies that provide interest and intrigue.

How you respond to these areas is deeply connected to who you are and how you respond to life. Sounds complex, but it is as clear as if you saw a pro basketball player in a small cottage room. You can't explain it—it just feels smothering. For others, a room too large threatens self-esteem, making one stand back in the corner, looking for comfort and control.

Some respond positively to large windows that connect them with nature. Others hurry to cover picture windows, finding daytime exposure and black glass at night overwhelming. A too-high ceiling can diminish self-confidence.

After you rethink the relationship between you and your home, and you realize the architecture isn't working with the decor, understand that it's a challenge that can be resolved.

Remember how you felt when you first saw the view from the French doors to the deck? Romance it with a comfortable chair and surround yourself with loved things.

When you look at an undressed room, the root of its appeal is obvious to you. If you can do this before you move in, it's very easy. Watch a family with three children walk into a new home, and each child will instinctively run to a bedroom and claim it. Children's instincts can teach us a few things. One likes to snuggle and chooses a small room with a small window. Another, probably the extrovert of the group, loves the room with the big corner windows that look onto the backyard. Another wants the room next to Mom and Dad's, for security.

So how do you clear the mental slate, especially if you're already living in the house? Take those floor plans and make lots of copies. Then start making notes. Don't worry about neatness. Write, mark, and draw what instantly comes to mind about each room. Use a yellow highlighter to shade in positive features. Write notes and trigger words. Use a blue highlighter on a separate copy to denote negative areas and features. Just be honest about what feels good or bad. While it's not realistic to think that you can make changes to rectify all these issues, what's important is to understand them and their effect on you, so you can furnish and decorate to compensate or complement.

IS YOUR HOUSE SENSITIVE TO YOUR NEEDS AND COMFORTS? Do I sense a wrinkling of the brow? If your house has any of these drawbacks, no wonder: ■ The living room window is off-center. ■ The ductwork has turned the ceilings into a maze of clipped corners and asymmetrical bulkheads. ■ The chandelier is centered in the dining room, not over the

A career artist would fall in love with the high-window light sources in this room. The challenge is to remember that and not relegate the "studio" to a back room.

dining room table because the builder didn't take into account putting a hutch on one side. ■ The front door is unsheltered so weather blasts into the foyer. ■ The bathroom is so small you have to back up to sit down. ■ The closets are tucked under staircases, making upper storage useless. ■ The kitchen has four doors and traffic snarls at key cooking times. ■ The tops of the windows in the family room aren't in line with the top of the sliding glass door, so coordinating window treatments seems impossible. ■ And last, but not least, is the corner fireplace next to a sliding glass door. Phew, now you know I read my fan mail! And, those little nooks that look so romantic in older homes become little devils to work with six months after you move in!

Reality: Rare is the house that is architectural genius, with line and form, balance, stunning lighting, comfort and practicality; very little furniture, drapery, or accessories would be needed. What happens in reality is decorating has to make up for architectural inadequacies, construction mistakes, and bad planning.

So, let's make the best of what you have, remembering the positives, making each room a part of your family's life in a meaningful way. Remember the features that spoke to you initially. Those are your markers to follow. A chandelier hanging in the wrong spot is simply a minor hiccup.

Big plants hide sins. A designer's "eraser" is a large plant! When the "archi-uglies"—tight corners, offset windows, ductwork boxes, and bulkheads—threaten the perfect space, we designers whip up the biggest potted plant we can find. Light permitting, a potted plant is easier, faster, and less expensive than a stud-and-wallboard or heavy drapery correction.

STEP 2

DETERMINE HOW YOU LIVE IN YOUR HOUSE. Take a good look at the way your family functions in your home. Not every family uses a house as the floor plan dictates.

THE ACTIVITY EXERCISE: Take another copy of your floor plan. On each room area, write all the activities that occur there and by whom. Is dinner in front of the TV or at a table? Does homework get done on the family room floor or at the kitchen table? Drop the room names and look at the functions. Does your furniture accommodate the *real* activity that occurs in the room, or is it there because of the expectations of the room's name? Bingo! This is expensive and *private* real estate you're furnishing! Are you decorating for the room or for your family's needs? Remember, decisions made for design's sake that go against your lifestyle will wear away at your contentment.

Now that I've really got you thinking, how far do you go? Do you turn the dining room into a sewing room because you sew there? Why preserve the formal dining room that's used only three times a year while you confine your true passion—sewing—to a closet-size cubby in the basement? Do you have the courage to make a change? SUGGESTION: Keep the dining room table, but swap the buffet for an armoire to hold sewing materials and equipment. Or add sheer curtains on the inside of the buffet's glass doors for material storage. Display the china on your walls. See where I'm going?

Make the best of what you have. Use the features that spoke to you initially as your markers.

Is the kitchen table "homework central"? Add a library. Pull your home office out of the dark back bedroom. Glam it up for the living room with a corner screen. Dining rooms make the best sewing rooms. Stash your notions and projects in an armoire. Libraries and living rooms are natural partners.

If you find this exercise difficult, take the names off the rooms on your floor plan. Think of them as boxes on paper you can rename any way you like. It's your home. You just might find that your living room should be the family room and the family room should be your office! *You deserve to love all of your home.*

STEP 3

IDENTITY YOUR FAVORITE PLACE. Here is an exercise that I conduct in many decorating clinics, and it is sure to get you thinking:

THE FAVORITE PLACE EXERCISE: Think of the one place where you most enjoy being in your house. Limit it to a 4x4-foot area. For instance, your favorite end of the sofa for reading, the bathtub in the morning with perfect light, your desk because it's private, or the rocking chair in the baby's room because it's peaceful. Think only of the place and the position you're in, not the entire room.

Write it down, then describe in a list of single words why that is your favorite space. If you don't have a place in your home that you feel good about, go in your mind's eye to another house, a restaurant, hotel, or your mother's home. Ask each member of your household to do the same thing. Don't walk around the house looking for this place; do it with your eyes closed so you dig into your memory bank of comfortable impressions. You

Create rooms by how you live, not on what the floor plan says.

Your favorite place may be the bedroom mid-afternoon because of the gorgeous light. Since mid-afternoon naps are impractical, take advantage of the view by adding an activity area such as a writing desk.

might take the family out for a picnic and bring pencils and paper so everyone gets involved without the immediate influence of the house as it looks today. If you ask these questions of your family in a more direct manner without the existing references, you usually get abstract answers, a shrug with "I don't care," and often "magazine house" dreams that can't apply to your existing home.

If the answers come quickly and they're specific, that tells me there's a big difference between your favorite spot and everyplace else. You need to go to work. If the answer comes slowly, ponderously, because you love being everywhere in your home, stop now and give this book to someone who needs it! You've done it. You don't need me! Too often one or two spots in a house are really perfect and the rest are just rooms with no heart displaying furniture.

If you can nominate more than one favorite place in your home, you're in good shape. Analyze all of them and you'll probably find some common factors. You may also find common elements between the favorite places of other family members too.

Bring the family together and ask each person to present their choice as if they are selling that spot to the others: how that place makes them feel, what they see—a view, a color, a picture on the wall. There is no silly reason for why you feel good somewhere. Sometimes you really have to think hard about the "why," but those answers are key to your understanding of your home and how you relate to it.

Exaggerate a bay. When you love a feature, emphasize it. In this case, a bay seemed tacked onto a moderate-size living room. Gathering the seating around its light brought the window seat into the conversation area. But the arrangement left awkwardly empty corners. Flanking the bay with bookshelves served to deepen its effect and eliminated the need for softening fabric side panels.

Remember, the place you choose should be instinctive, a first reaction. The selling part is a hoot! Lots of laughs. You'll learn a lot about your home and even about your spouse and kids—things you never knew they were sensitive to.

The result is a list of favorite uses, colors, details, furniture, lighting, and space—all relating to what you already have. This is a really honest start.

Go for the antithesis: Think of your least-favorite place. Again, write it down along with your reasons in a list of single words. Have each member of your family do this too. This time it's a complaint session. (Keep to the subject at hand! A plea for the car keys on Friday, or chore negotiation, is off-base.)

Wow, this is powerful. What do you do with this information? The objective is to make *all* of your home your family's haven. You and they have the right and opportunity *to love all of it.*

Now, take the single word descriptions of those favorite places and apply them to the places everyone likes least. Can you take those qualities of the favorites and apply them in some way—a treatment, a color, a new light fixture, a comfortable chair, even renovation—to the least-favorite places? The answer isn't absolute. But you'll have a much better understanding of why you retreat to certain areas and conditions.

Too often one or two spots in your house are really perfect and the rest are just rooms displaying furniture with no heart.

It's just a simple kitchen desk, but it's a favorite place. No matter how mundane compared to the more obvious architectural features of the house, if you love the spot make it important with your favorite, even important accessories like this designer chair and fresh flowers.

I can see how someone would love to sit at this kitchen table facing the window—a favorite place. It's bright and I find myself delighted by the bright harvest colors in the upholstery fabric on the bench seat. Now, take that harvest gold and deepen it to a caramel—and don't chicken out—make an all-white bathroom. There is so much white that the bold color serves as an accent. Again, this room has lots of light to bring it to life. Simplify the accessories and this is the perfect place for a decadent mid-afternoon soak.

should be your favorite."

TRANSLATING HOW YOU FEEL INTO DECOR TREATMENTS AND SOLUTIONS IS ACTUALLY EASY:

HOW YOU'D LIKE A SPACE TO FEEL:	*Do This:*
COZIER	*Add richer color, larger scale furnishings, a larger coffee table, larger lamps, heavier window treatments, lots of pillows.*
ROOMIER	*Expose lots of wall area, choose lower profile furniture, undersized area rugs, under-accessorize with fewer bolder items, frame pictures with wide mats.*
HAPPIER	*Build a color scheme based on brights and clear colors. Use a sense of humor in your accessories.*
QUIETLY ELEGANT	*Use easy-on-the-eye monochromatic schemes, mix classical styles with artful "finds." Naturals are a cinch.*

Although I can't describe every emotional reaction to a room, these give you a start.

Now blend all of your thoughts and reactions into a plan. Just because a favorite spot is in a bright yellow room doesn't mean the whole house should be painted yellow. Perhaps you love yellow because of the uplifting light. There are versions of all the colors that will give a similar happy look. In a corner that's a least-favorite place, a yellow chair, a yellow painted stool, or a yellow accessory will improve your reaction to the space.

The trick to moving a favorite color around a house without boring repetition is to connect color schemes from room to room through trading places of importance between major and minor colors. For more help on choosing colors, refer to my color system in *Straight Talk on Decorating.*

"cozy" "roomy"

"happy" "elegant"

BAIT

STEP 4

GETTING TO KNOW YOU, GETTING TO LIKE YOU. Our perception of how we live is often different from reality and that's where a designer would find a disconnect between how you dream of living in your home and what you say you are dissatisfied with.

For example, you see yourself as an ordered, reserved, quiet type—and your home is anything but: disconnected spaces, loungy furniture, and unorganized storage systems. And someone whose life is freewheeling, an anything-goes type, might find themselves with uptight traditional furniture in an elegant wallpapered manse that they keep for sentimental and status reasons. First, let's get honest about who we really are. You can't fool your psyche into living something you're not. It will make you crazy.

I'll use myself as an example. As a designer I can make virtually any house into nearly any style of living. I love the ballet of minimalism. So I once underdecorated a home into a white-and-natural composition of line and form. Everything was perfectly placed: a single amaryllis to the left of a pair of candlesticks on the left side of the asymmetrical mantel arrangement, to offset the perfectly propped stained

The objective is to love all of your home.

glass mirror...*you get the picture*. Could I put a birthday card from my daughter on the mantel? Good heavens, no. It would mess with the balance. Could I drop my keys, mail, and purse on the glass dining table with the floating orchid and candle arrangement slightly off to the side? Good grief, it would be a horrible color contrast! Well, I have all due respect for people who can live this way, because they have much more restraint than I do. I loved the elegance, the control, the simplicity—it was gorgeous—with lots of WOW factor. Friends, party guests, even the bug man loved being there. Parts of it were peaceful, but it was TOO PEACEFUL! It made me crazy because I simply do not live that way. I'm not sloppy, just too busy with no time for perfection. So I got honest with myself: No matter how much I love the look, only a shoehorn could wedge my life into that style. Bad fit.

Let's first get honest about who we really are. You can't fool your psyche into living something you're not. It will make you crazy.

My house is a rambling stone and wood Western homestead. All colors and styles thrown together. Totally casual. Guests and family coming and going nonstop. Nothing stays in the same place more than a week. Relaxed? Yes. Fun? Absolutely. Everyone who visits remarks how peaceful the place is!

EVALUATE YOUR LIVING STYLE. This is another step in helping you really think about some of your choices. We all love a lot of different things, and our preferences often change over time. Ask women how they feel about their wedding china! Sometimes jarring contrasts show up. One day you like the austere Zen look, and then you go on holiday in Montana and become enamored with the decor in a cowboy bar. What gives with that? And how can you pick a style to live with when all these things appeal to you?

The benefit of the MY STYLE EXERCISE is to help expose your *true* likes and keep you grounded with what you're living in and with. Therein lies the real, the feel-good, the practical and affordable answers. And all will culminate in your uncompromising, personal, "my way" style.

WHAT'S YOUR LIFESTYLE? HOW DO YOU LIVE?

THE MY STYLE EXERCISE:

After each question, I've put some ideas to get you thinking, but if your choice isn't mentioned or you've got a twist, place a few self-stick notes on the page, and write down your answer: Personal choice is what this exercise is all about!

1. Do you dress up for work every day? (i.e. suit and tie, suit and heels)? Do you dress casual for work (slacks and shirt, skirts and blouses)? Or do you dress in a practical way for the work you do (khakis, jeans, shirts, track suits)?

2. How do you dress when you get home (stay in your work clothes, switch to jeans or khakis, get in athletic mode with track clothes, or simply retire for the evening in your jammies)?

3. What is dinner time like (on the run, at the kitchen counter, at the kitchen table, in the dining room, watching TV, out at a restaurant, or in the car on the way home from work)? Think about the weekdays, and also about the weekends; you may find a big difference.

4. Where do you relax (in the kitchen, the living room, in the family room with the kids, outdoors, working in the garage, in front of the TV, relaxing in the bedroom, a hobby area, sewing room, etc.), or don't you have the time to relax?

5. How much time do you spend in the bathroom (just for necessities, doing personal grooming and dressing, or lounging, spa, whirlpool tub etc.)?

6. How do you use your bedroom (for sleeping and dressing only, for lounging, as a home office, or for reading)?

7. How do you use your living room (for formal occasions only, every day, as a quiet zone, to play with kids, or never — it's a showplace only)?

8. How do you use your dining room (dinner every day, formal occasions only, to sort the mail, as a home office, for crafts, or a place to do kids' projects)?

9. When you come and go from the house, where do you drop your coats, keys, purse, and mail (at the front door, the back door, in the kitchen, or near the garage)?

10. What do you drive (a car, minivan, SUV, truck)?

11. What do you do for fun? What's your favorite activity?

12. Take a look in your closet. What category do the majority of your clothes fall into: casual, semi-casual, semi-formal, formal?

PLACE YOUR STICKIES HERE

"and where do you live?"

CONCLUSION:

After going through the questions, it becomes pretty clear which lifestyle you're leaning toward. Although I refer to it as *your* lifestyle, it really includes your whole family's style of living. However, one of you tends to lead.

You remember why you fell in love with your house, pinpointed wonderful features and problem spots. You've identified a favorite place and the elements of favorite places, and taken a look at how you live. Next, we'll fit what you have (furnishings, accessories, and "stuff") into your new ideas. Reality check!

Understanding the elements that make a place a favorite is very important.

The hardest part of design is analyzing the emotional and practical responses to space, then translating that information into color, upholstery, and wood. This is what the pros do. It's typically a long process—and you've just done it yourself!

If a designer walked in and asked, "What's your style?" You'd say, "What style? What I have is a collection of things; it's not American or Modern. Besides I wouldn't know a 'Louis the Whatzit' if I was sitting on it!" We all have a mixed collection. Good for us—it's the diversity of our collections that gives our homes individuality and intrigue. In design, it's the ultimate freedom. Unless you're a collector or studied afficionado of a particular period, nix the style labels.

It's far more important to declare your *life*style, because it's the true root of your design *style*: what you like *about* color, comfort, views, furniture, etc.

P.S. Don't forget that the kids have favorite places too. A window seat is the perfect place for dreaming of faraway adventures. Give them their own private window seat as well—flank the bedroom window with bookshelves and build a bench underneath. Make it as deep as you dare and add lots of soft cushions.

"Identify what you love...

"I didn't know I liked green until I realized that my pottery collection was my favorite thing."
That's the kind of cue you're looking for. Then simply add more of what you like. The dusty-
green room trimmed with white gives the same soothing impression as the white with green
pottery. Mother Nature pairs green with every blooming color—and so should you!

then repeat it."

SORT YOUR STUFF
START YOUR PLAN

START WITH WHAT YOU ALREADY HAVE. You can't decorate using your current things as a base unless you can look at them objectively. THE LOVE IT OR LEAVE IT EXERCISE is where your personal style—the results of everything we've worked on up to now—meets what you have: your furniture, accessories, collections, and stuff.

Meld your personal style with the stuff you have—It's a big job that starts with major sorting.

The primary category is furniture and accessories you have been collecting for a while. The second category is what I call *stuff*. For the sporting, it's the gear. For the crafter, it's boxes of materials. For the gardener, it's pots, trays, and tools. For young parents, it's toys, swings, playpens, and plastic everywhere. For the empty nester it's books, photographs, and memorabilia. This *stuff* is what you rarely see in decorating magazines, books, and shows, but it is a big part of your life. Everyone whose "perfect" house has been photographed has closets and a back bedroom where all the stuff has been shoved

The objective: To live with only what you love.

into hiding for the photo shoot day! The perfect decorating that has become the model is completely unrealistic. "Stuff" is 50 percent of real life. (*Do I hear applause?*)

What is your "stuff"? If you're a crafter, it's materials and tools. If you're a gardener, it's pots and trowels that need a place. If you have kids, it's toys, swings, playpens, etc. And if you love to travel the seas, your souvenirs are your "stuff" and deserve to be displayed in a proper place.

STEP 1

RENEW YOUR OBJECTIVITY. Far above every whine, complaint, and dilemma, redecorating is the apology for one's furnishings. "Mixed up, doesn't go, too old, too new," and worst of all, "I love it but it doesn't work." Why? Probably because you're trying to fit a lifelong collection into a magazine image. We need to clean the canvas again and take a fresh look at what you have and *love*. The primary objective of this exercise is to realize what you really love and plan to live with only those items. Why be surrounded with things that subconsciously put bad karma in your day? Don't be frightened. We're not replacing everything in your house.

THE LOVE IT OR LEAVE IT EXERCISE. Document in a photo file every piece of furniture you own. Take the pictures catalog-style as shown below. No context, just the furniture. Be sure to photograph everything. Do not edit at this point. No decision making. Even if you think you'll never use the dresser in the back bedroom, take the picture.

OPPOSITE: Here's an unusual example of loved items: a collection of cobbler forms. The tiny one on top of two books and a candlestand elevates it to a place of honor among other items that are important to this family. Its simple utility is now sculptural.

This is an objective, not a subjective, process. Then, get prints of the photos and on the back make notes of color, imperfections, repair needed, etc. Next, both you and your partner separately (with no discussion) sort the pictures into three categories. It's important to do this individually: You'll learn more about each other's honest appraisals! You just might find that instead of the *"Whatever you want, honey"* response, you'll get a real reaction.

Now comes the most important step—so be brutally honest. Sort your pictures with an instant reaction into three piles. Don't think too long about each photo. CATEGORY 1 **Love It!** *Wouldn't live without it.* CATEGORY 2 **So-So...** *Serves a purpose, but would replace it if you could afford it.* CATEGORY 3 **Leave It.** *Never did like it. Gone!*

Love It!	**So-So...**	**Leave It.**

 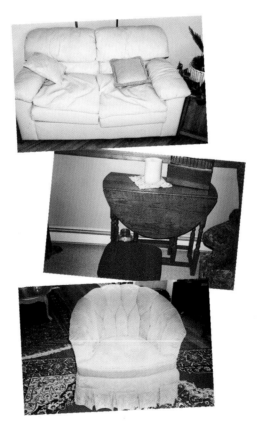 

NOW, LET'S SEE WHAT WE CAN LEARN FROM THIS

CATEGORY 1 Love It! Look at your pictures in this category. Why do you love those pieces? Color, shape, comfort, sentimental attachment, status? Consider the photos one at a time: Is it the color? Does the color elicit a certain mood? Is it delicious, exciting, handsome, sexy, easy? Answer these questions and you'll start to get somewhere. Is it the shape? Graceful, strong, simple, complicated? Is it the comfort? Does it make you sit upright or lounge? Is it great for reading, watching TV, chatting?

Or is it a sentimental thing? If so, is it only the sentiment that makes you keep it, or does it have a secondary appeal? Remember that just because it was your grandfather's rocker doesn't mean you have to use it. It can work as an art piece to be admired, contributing to the mood and personality of a room. But if guilt is a factor, give it to another family member.

Now, look at the descriptions and reasons you love what you have and marry these concepts to what you learned about your true personal style. See the connections?

CATEGORY 2 So-So... Hmmmm...This category is tough. You don't hate the items in here, but you don't love them either. They serve a purpose. Maybe you're attached to a few of these items. But they don't have any effect on how you feel about a room. They don't add anything. What a wasted opportunity! Everything in your visual bubble should contribute to making a great, favorite place. Think of these items as eventually on their way out, or to be repainted or reupholstered.

Are you worried that you won't be able to find a replacement that you love? That isn't a good reason to keep something: You *will* find something now that you know what you need to look for. Keeping your radar up is half the process. Whether you find the replacement soon or a year from now, remember that these items are on their way out the door either for resale or to be recycled into a lovable item.

Whatever you do, don't move these pictures into the "Love It!" pile. Trust your first instincts. Investigate consignment shops, auctions, and local higher-end garage, tag, and estate sales. You may be surprised what some items are worth. Sell three or four items in the "So-So..." pile and you may be able to afford one fabulous item. *Remember your objective:* To live with only what you love, even if for the time being you have a little and not a lot.

> **Is a favorite item sentimental but not useful? Not everything you love has to be useful; you can display it just to enjoy it.**

CATEGORY 3 **Leave It.** Out, out, out! Unless you risk having a totally naked room, sleeping on the floor, or eating on the kitchen counter, get rid of anything you hate—now! Don't make another decorating decision until those items have disappeared! The daily negative vibes just aren't worth it. And worst of all, the influence these things have on your ongoing creative decision making process is deadly. Dreadfully distracting. They'll pull you in the wrong direction.

If you must live with something for now, make it tolerable. If it's a table that's staying at the risk of having nothing, cover it with a favorite tablecloth. If it's a bed, invest in the most beautiful bed coverings you can afford. If it's the sofa, go right this minute to purchase a slipcover. The financial investment in the temporary fixes is worth more than I can describe. You simply can't choose a good wall color when

Anything and everything is a candidate for the wall! That's my motto. I love the courage in free-hanging the silver service inside this heavy frame. One arrangement like this can say so much about you, your home, the room, and your sense of humor.

hovering nearby is a nasty-color sofa you're planning to get rid of.

Get rid of everything in "Leave It!" that you can possibly live without. Sell it at a garage sale. You're better off living with less than you are living with the aggravation of seeing stuff you don't like. With the items from this category gone, at least you'll be looking at a fresh start. And with luck, the money from the garage sale will buy one more gorgeous piece to add to your "Love It!" collection. You don't need much in a room to make it decorated. If the room feels naked, fill it with color.

If you must live with it for now, make it lovable. The financial investment in the temporary fixes is worth more than I can describe.

Imagine how this favorite place may have been created: Perhaps the chair was iffy, but the loose-fitting slipcover raised its cache, or the lamp was a curbside salvage piece that only needed a fancy shade to fit in. Perhaps the decor started with the accessories—the creamy colored vases, worn-whites furniture, and buttery fabrics. Move the chair to the window, and it's a favorite place filled with "Love It!" things.

A NOTE ON COLOR

Ooopppss. There's that word again. The dreaded "color" so flippantly, nonchalantly used by decorators and feared to the core by everyone else. Go back to the green chest and red cushion, or how about all the red accessories in your wardrobe. But those hide in the closet and the wall is out there for the world to see. Hey, who is the world? This is *your* house we're talking about! Get a brush and get to it. Just don't pick the color in the paint store; pick the color at home. Find something in your closet, a page torn from a magazine (and not of a room) or a square inch of color from an ad, or a flower. Take that to the store to be color-matched by computer. If you stand at the paint chip display trying to decide, I guarantee you'll come home with off-white and a headache, and an ache in your psyche—the guilt of settling for safe but oh-so-boring again.

The lesson here is to think of color the same way you're learning to think about your "stuff"—live with only what you love and change the things that compromise your style. If a room's color doesn't suit you, then the whole room can't ever be your style.

Find your favorite thing in the whole house— one that makes you smile. Use it for inspiration.

If you're uncomfortable being really bold with color, try painting just one wall in a room a bold color. Don't decide right away whether you like it; live with the color for at least a week.

Just one big picture—say a favorite from Grandmother's house—in a place of honor is all you need to decorate a room and add color. Put it on a wall by itself where you can see it frequently as you move from room to room, and paint the wall or the whole room a color that makes the picture stand out; these walls are the soft peachy-pink tone of the water lilies. You can also make a picture feel bolder by complementing it with other items, like framing it with candle sconces. Just be careful that the other items don't distract.

STEP 2

THE FANNY-FRIENDLY EXERCISE. This has to do with editing your "Love It!" pile for comfort. This is the most important element of furniture decision making for me. Out of a hundred drop-dead gorgeous chairs, only one is going to fit my fanny just so. Be stubborn about this test. REMEMBER: Is the furniture there to make the house look good or to make you feel good?

Sit in each sofa, loveseat, and chair for an entire evening after dinner. One

*There should be no bad seats in your house....**all seats must be comfortable!***

seating piece each night. Since you probably don't sit down all evening every evening, this may take some time. Read, watch TV, chat, or listen to music—the activity really doesn't matter as long as you are absorbed in something. Now give that seating piece a comfort rating from 1 to 10. A rating of 1 is "Can't wait to do something else and get out of here." And 10 is "Hand me my teddy bear and go away world, I'm home."

Anything above a 5 is worth keeping. Price anything below a 5 for a garage sale because clearly it was selected or purchased for looks and not livability. Or maybe your lifestyle changed, and you grew out of the pieces. You know there's a problem when friends bypass the living room to find a spot in the kitchen. Yes, the kitchen is the heart of the home, but it's nice to have a comfy place to enjoy a glass of wine, a hearth area with great chairs to sink into, and a sofa that fits a Saturday afternoon nap. The average American home has a ground floor with kitchen, living room,

The comfort rating of this grouping absolutely jumps out at you. A perfect 10. All snugged up to a fireplace that's full of warmth and charm, the grouping almost sings with coziness and conviviality. And the generously stuffed sofa and wing chair surely pass the comfort test!

"Repeat...no

...ad seats in your house. "

This eclectic gathering of seating pieces looks like a lively conversation all by itself—what could be more inviting? Each piece practically begs you to sit down and make yourself at home. Think of the conviviality and inviting nature of your seating pieces. If your chairs or sofas are more off-putting than inviting, it's time to either replace them or revive them with new slipcovers or cushions.

dining room, and powder room of 1,000 to 1,800 square feet. If one-third of it is all you use, no matter how inviting your kitchen, something is seriously wrong. If you have a living room/dining room/foyer and powder room that are rarely used, that's expensive real estate just for show. And who are you showing it off to? Your friends don't want to be there!

DECISION TIME

There should be no bad seats in your house; they must be comfortable, have a resting place for books and mug, be oriented to another seat for conversation, and, this is very important, have something interesting, calming, relaxing, or beautiful to look at.

Place the most important piece of seating where you most like to look.

How many ways can you place your sofa? Go back to sitting in your chairs, the comfort rating, and why you love it. I'm sure the rating had something to do with what you were looking at. Place the sofa, the most important seating piece, where you most like to look. Now go through this exercise with the next most important seating piece and its position. Here's the first bump. Only have one good side of the room to look at? Possibly out of the main window or toward the fireplace? Well, now you have to make something pretty to look at for those seated in the other chairs.

Are you a minimalist? Can you live with less? Simple color, bold lines, and lots of texture all contribute to creating a peaceful feeling. For some, this is a gentle, cozy conversation area. For others this room—although appreciated for its style—would be maddeningly restrictive.

CONCLUSION

After these exercises, you're probably feeling scared, unsettled. Did we just turn your house inside out? Maybe. But now you know your home better than before. You remember why you love its features and imperfections. You're centered on your true instincts about your interior world. You've learned more about your family's reactions to their house. A few surprises, perhaps? Now that you have a clear picture of what you need, you have the guts to start creating The Plan. You have a filter through which to pass furniture, colors, and magazine inspirations. No more confusion. Now it's just the delights of choice.

Go at this process over time, as you can afford it. But never forget your instinctive responses to your surroundings. Make only choices that fit you—and, above all—NO COMPROMISE. *Promise?*

If you've taken the steps in my exercise, then you're on your way to No Compromise decorating.

Forget "precious." That's for show and doesn't live. Says designer James, "A room where you can't put your feet up is just a pretty room." Does that rule out hard-core Traditional? No, just choose good-quality materials. Fabrics with lots of detail and distressed wood furniture is much more kidproof than much of the austere, modern plastics of that era so trendy today. The exposed hardwood floors and bright yellow on the walls relax this room full of formal pieces.

"So, does your room

Favorite place? The cushy end of the sofa for is for reading. Made a library that "recessed" the window into a faux bay. The room that romanced the house? The sun room on the back of the house—now this living room! What's in the old living room at the front of the house? Use your imagination!

it you and your lifestyle?"

NO COMPROMISE DECORATING WHAT IF

SCARED? TAKE A DEEP BREATH AND TRUST YOUR INSTINCTS. Most people are a little scare as they dip that paintbrush into a fresh can of color. It's not unlike an actor's butterflies while waiting in the wings. Some say it's those butterflies that ensure a peak performance. It's the adrenaline that keeps you focused and excited. It should be exciting, especially if you KNOW without a doubt who you are and what you want, and now have the opportunity to finally do it!

Decorating should be exciting, so don't get hung up on the little things.

YOUR QUESTION *But what if I hate what I've done? It's a big mistake? I'm worried what everyone else will think...*

MY RESPONSE You won't feel this way if you've been honest about your responses in our exercises. Remember the name of this book. You promised! NO COMPROMISE. Decorating is an art and not a science. Every home, homeowner, furniture collection, lighting condition, and budget is different. No two are alike. That's why I don't like decorating rules. How can any rule fit every situation? Impossible. The most important thing to remember is that you are unique. Your taste and eye for beauty are unique. And this is your home, no one else's.

The most important thing to remember is that you are unique. Your taste and eye for beauty are unique. And this is your home, no one else's.

Change takes an adjustment. Live with what you've done for a bit. Don't panic. Within a few days, you'll settle into your true "look" and love it, like an old shoe. All because now it's really, really you!

An old table surrounded by unmatched chairs: The combination is inviting. Unhung pictures and a column in the corner further loosen the arrangement. But the kicker is the combination striped-and-floral curtains; cover them with your hand to see the difference without them.

YOUR QUESTION *My spouse and I can't agree. We came up with opposite answers and reactions to your exercises! What now?*

MY RESPONSE Good question. Actually I found myself in the same situation. My husband's answers were quite different from mine. But that's OK. The ideal is for each member of the house to have a favorite spot in each and every common room. That's not hard to accomplish. My husband has a favorite chair and I have a favorite end of the sofa. Are our color preferences similar? No. He loves really rich dense blues and I prefer dusty naturals. So I work our colors together. Sometimes the blues are accents in a natural-themed room; and in rooms where he spends the most time, I've used his

Your home is a reflection of your partnership, and it should be a celebration of that uniqueness.

palette as a primary theme, softening the hard blues with natural accents. Our furniture preferences are also very different. He prefers substantial shapes and I like more intricate designs. The contrast is wonderful and gives our home a uniqueness that's wonderfully interesting. And that's the key to your answer. Your partnership is a unique coupling of personalities and approaches to life. And because your home is a reflection of that partnership, it too will be a celebration of that uniqueness. I would expect to find an eclectic decor in your home, as interesting to visit as you are as a couple. The "matchy-matchy" totally coordinated house is not for you. Flow with the differences. Much more fun.

Quick—what's your gut reaction to this room? Then get your spouse's instant reaction. Chances are you both had different reactions to the space. While I love the serenity of the neutrals, my husband wouldn't like the unflinching white palette, but we might both like the elegant pieces in the room. So a little more color for him and we'd have a room we could both enjoy.

YOUR QUESTION *We're moving in the next couple of years. How important is it that we decorate to this specific house and what will happen when we move to the next? We can't afford to start over.*

MY RESPONSE Your reaction to your current home and favorite places is really an exercise to teach you about your reactions to specific architectural features. That actually doesn't change as you move from one place to another. If your favorite place is by a certain window, it's most likely because of the light or view. When you move to the next house, you will almost surely be drawn to a similar situation somewhere in some room. It's your comfort in that certain spot that you are using for the basis of decoration, colors, upholstery, and pictures. Those preferences follow you as you move. Your favorite spot by the den window in the previous house will guide you to look in the next house for that special place that makes you feel good—possibly by the window in the breakfast area or living room.

It's your comfort in a room, in a certain spot that you use for the basis of your choice in decoration, colors, upholstery, and pictures.

And as for your furniture, you'll keep it with you. Other than adding and subtracting for "fit" purposes, your collection is the guts of your personal style. Rearrange and re-sort it into the various rooms. This is an opportunity to shake it up a little. A dresser from a previous bedroom may end up as a buffet in the kitchen. An armoire from the guest bedroom might find a new position as a linen cabinet in the upstairs hall. But it's all still totally you. If you need new things, remember to wait and buy only what you *love* and not just something to fill the space or immediate need. NO COMPROMISE!

Your furniture and accessories move with you as a unit of personal style. Modernist furniture and simple dressing doesn't look the least bit comfortable in this rustic setting. Undressing the windows and flattening the room color put the emphasis on the red accents.

YOUR QUESTION *My taste keeps changing. If I were wealthy, it wouldn't be a problem. But on my budget, how do I keep up with my decorating "hobby"? I get so bored so fast.*

MY RESPONSE If this is the real you and decorating really is a favorite pastime, be honest with it. First step is to create a base of flexible furniture. By this I mean multipurpose pieces like armoires, side tables, and really comfortable club chairs. Don't match anything. And invest in these good-quality anchors in a variety of styles and wood grains. Now you have an eclectic base. With this you can go anywhere

One of my favorite tricks is to utilize two-sided throw pillows to flip when my mood changes.

with colors, patterns, and accessories. Limit spending on accessories. This is your playground. Now you can swing from contemporary to traditional with very little investment and not feel wasteful or guilty doing it. My favorite tricks: two-sided throw pillows to flip with my mood, optional lamp shades for each base—one rustic and one fine silk, or iron table bases with separate tops so I can change from glass to wood to stone. Of course, there are always slipcovers for total quick-change upholstery.

Decorating is an art and not a science. Every home, homeowner, furniture collection, lighting condition, and budget are different. That's why I don't like decorating rules.

A room full of good furniture in neutral colors is like a canvas: You can overlay almost any style on it. Imagine these shelves filled with books instead of pottery, wool pillows in deep browns and burgundies instead of a leopard print, and a black shade on the lamp—and this room becomes a cocooning library rather than an airy sitting room.

GO FOR IT

DEAR FRIEND,

My mission in writing NO COMPROMISE was to stop you before you make another scary color decision and to make you hesitate before you buy another piece of furniture because you need it now and it's the only one in stock. I want you to decorate because you *love* the purchase you are about to make and are not afraid of it. I want you to be convinced that what you are about to do, you will do from a vision that you are confident about. Being scared and nervous every time you go shopping is not how it should be. *Is it right? Will it "go"? Is it too wild? Will he like it? What if everyone thinks it's silly? Will they take it back? What if I hate it in two weeks and I've spent all this money?* If that's what improving your home is all about, everyone should live in beige and white because the case of nerves just isn't worth it.

Take style labels, trends, and the old decorating rules away from the process; take a fresh look at your home and how you live in it.

Take style labels, trends, and the old decorating "rules" away from the process. Take a fresh look at your home and how you live in it. Be honest about what you like and dislike about your furniture and accessories. Be brutally honest. And then act. That's sometimes the hard part: working up the courage to edit, to take that first step, and possibly to live without a few things for a while. But the process and the end result of a home that fits you like your favorite sneakers, that is all you, without compromise, is well...you'll see.

In each of these rooms, you can see a bit of a particular style—a little country, a touch of modern, whatever—but what's even more evident is the comfort and individuality of each space. These are rooms "designed" to accommodate busy lives and personal tastes. As soon as you start putting your decorating plan into action, you'll start to see the same elements appear in your room.

Here is what really happens when people like yourself follow my No Compromise decorating plan—when 10 everyday homeowners do the sort of their furniture, find a way to re-romance their homes, and rediscover their favorite places.

The exercises in this book are designed to help you organize the redecorating of your home, starting with what you already have. Use all the exercises, or use just those that give you confidence.

We followed ten homeowners as they went through the **No Compromise** process with my supervision and support. We had a blast!

- A teacher, her husband, who runs his business our of their home, and their two children found color and personality hiding in the accessories tucked away in upstairs bedrooms.

- Another couple rearranged their oversize, totally matched furniture to make room for the antiques they loved but thought didn't go.

- One family, conversely, found a way to pull together their mismatched collection of furniture and eclectic souvenirs.

- A quilt maven and her husband with their three teenagers, now find their large living room inviting with a new colors and walls covered with memories and quilts.

- Our retired couple's 1960s suburban ranch got a whole new kitchen using just color and her collectibles. (Clearly, these exercises aren't just for living

I want the homeowners to make every room lovable and livable. The solution for each home, however, is different. You can't use a one-size-fits-all approach and expect individualized results!

rooms and dens!)

■ Young parents, with a toddler in tow and a baby on the way, did a French country makeover on their kitchen.

■ The hand-me-downs in a young bachelor's starter home got re-sorted into a high-design, very hip, facelift for less than $500. Only a very few items actually got relegated to the "Leave It" pile.

Every homeowner I worked with had to put in study time to understand both home and needs. And each of them came away with not only great rooms but a better understanding of themselves.

■ A huge impact was achieved in two larger projects where homeowners actually used the results of these exercises to launch major renovations. One couple even added a staircase in the middle of an L-shape living/dining space to provide access to a new second-story master bedroom. And the new colors, a new sofa, and curbside finds transformed this Craftsman-style treasure for an active family with twins.

■ The second empty-nester couple had a wealth of beautiful antiques—everything they needed—but it was all in the wrong rooms! We scrambled their belongings to create a gorgeous wine-country manse.

As you can see, these exercises—my approach to solving your decorating challenges no matter the room—are all about rediscovering your romance with your home, remember how you really live in it, and renewing your objectivity with the things you love. Our homeowners and I welcome you to enjoy these real-life case studies.

THE CHALLENGE A home that's too sterile for them to feel comfortable in. **LYNETTE'S SOLUTION** Take the rigidity out of their furniture arrangement and warm up the rooms with contrasting color and texture. Bring out their favorite memories that are hidden away.

Janet and Ross, 30-somethings, with sons Liam, 8, and Haydon, 6, live in a small builder home. The house has good furniture but no warmth or personality. I asked what they liked most about their home, they replied—"Its potential. We know a lot can be done to give it a less-sterile feel. It is a home our family loves, and we would love to make it more 'ours.'"

Tell me your favorite place in the house. "We love the family room—it's comfortable and warmer than the other rooms. But still not 'ours.' It's almost there. Just a little too new looking." We can fix that.

Tell me your least favorite place. "The living room—not warm at all. We rarely use it." What a shame! You have well-chosen furniture—stylish, handsome. Your room just needs a twist. It was clear from the beginning that this family loved their home and had pretty, stylish accessories. But their fear of "doing something wrong" had frozen them into neutral colors that go with everything. And, this is a small home with no "extra" space, so everyone pretty much sees every room, every day. I went searching through the house for family treasures. Things that were happy memories. Just moving the Mickey Mouse print into the living room to the first wall you see when you enter makes you smile.

Their fear of "doing something wrong" had frozen them into neutral colors.

It's now a happy place. When we finished, Ross brought the kids home from school. They were wowwed. "Wait 'til Mom sees this!" He couldn't believe the transformation cost nearly nothing, and Janet just loved it. "Now we will use the living room. It's so much more friendly."

Love It!

So-So...

Love It !

■ Janet and Ross invested in some good, long-term pieces when they bought their home. They chose neutrals, but fell into a common trap: The Blahs. Even the handsome plaid wasn't enough to enliven the room. The good news: They have strong basics, good clean lines to work with.

■ The family room was over furnished with an oversize sectional and symmetrical TV unit. This was tough since the fireplace was cornered. They fought in scale, shape, and color: The white fireplace was diminished by the bulk of the darker wall unit. The answer was to integrate the fireplace into the wall unit with accessories, treating them as one large display.

■ Matching furniture can be a challenge. It cleans up a space visually; there's little disruption when neutral fabrics visually melt into the background. It can make the room seem larger. However, without interruption, the neutrality works against you. I found interesting accents to add color and personality.

So-So...

■ Janet wasn't crazy about the wood pieces, but wasn't sure why. They weren't the problem; in that neutral environment, the pieces didn't add anything. Now, in their perked-up setting, their shapes, forms, and texture become noticeable.

How We Did It

■ First, I had to get a handle on the whole room. It's just the right size to be cozy, but lacked spunk. Matching furniture can do that: All the upholstery matched, all of the tables matched. Other than the Mickey Mouse print and two framed scenic images picked up on holiday, nothing said this room belonged to this family.

■ To loosen up the arrangement, make it more personable, we angled the sofa and loveseat enough to visually reshape the room. To give the corner height, we put the palm plant up on a bench.

■ The rocking chair in tan/black plaid became more important in its new, more obvious corner. It is the "character" piece in the grouping, but it was hiding in plain sight. Now you see it as you enter the room and it says, "Come in and chat." Rocking chairs always say that!

■ The show wall, the first wall you see when entering a room, now has some excitement with an asymmetrical grouping of pictures, lamp, and table.

My favorite, the little antique chair, makes the room. This is the surprise piece I found in an upstairs guest bedroom where it was rarely seen. It's a wonderful example of how just one item, something with history, can shake up a neutral collection. Above all, it added that needed personal touch.

BEFORE

Janet and Ross's Challenge The family room simply lacked punch.

Lynette's Solution Their favorite accessory was the DIJON Bicyclettes poster. I asked if they had been to France. "No, we just loved the colors in the print." That was the cue I needed.

■ The addition of reds and golds to this very neutral setting was the answer. Vases, candlesticks, and plants. We hit the stores for red vases, candlesticks, and pillows. We re-sorted their photographs and ditched the dried flower arrangement; it was much too drab when we were looking for snap!

■ I found an exotic brass pouring set in their bedroom for the coffee table, a keepsake from the Far East that didn't get much notice; now it's a centerpiece that prompts curious inquiries.

■ **A NOTE ABOUT PILLOWS:** These days many new sofas come with throw pillows, sometimes six or eight pillows to form the back of the sofa. You don't have to use only those pillows. Mix those pillows with an assortment of new ones to add new colors to a room.

Their favorite print gave me the color cue I needed.

BEFORE

Cluster accessories when you're working with less.

Janet and Ross's Challenge The kitchen is a big blah. "Help, we're on a tight budget!"

Lynette's Solution I would have liked to tile the backsplash for color, but that wasn't in the immediate plan. This is a two-career, very busy household. So a quick trick was to hang plates. They add color, even pattern, and are easy to clean. When Janet and Ross are ready to tile or paper, they can recycle the dish collection elsewhere in the house.

BEFORE

THE CHALLENGE New home, with new furniture–but nearly not enough. How to fill space until the budget catches up. **LYNETTE'S SOLUTION** Cluster what you have to make the room warm. Invest in interesting multi-purpose accent pieces that you can use anywhere later.

Deanne and Dag with sons, Max, 4, and Sam, 1½, live in a custom-built home overlooking red-rock views. After I found out that petite Deanne's favorite spot was the corner of the family-room sectional, the reason for her reaction to the living room was obvious.

Her least-favorite place: "The living room because it's big and empty and I don't know what to do with it." Dag, a businessperson who works from his office at home, Deanne, and their two preschool boys share an open-concept plan from morning to night daily. That's a lot of lifestyle pressure in a seemingly wall-less floor plan. "Pods" of space and usage are really important here: Dad's need for privacy and quiet come by way of French doors. The kids need play space and Mom needs to manage the balance and still find a place for herself.

The sofa, table, and area rug was an island with walking space all around.

The living room wasn't being used at all and it had the primary view!

They had already edited their furniture before the movers came. Smart: What we had to work with was what they wanted to keep. So, rather than a furniture edit exercise, I asked them how they would prefer to use their "pods."

The floor plan is well-thought out. The common rooms are beautifully oriented to a view of the Colorado National Monument. But there was one major challenge—the living room. Because it was the center of the whole plan, all rooms lead from it with the foyer directly in front. The result is the feeling of no walls—just a giant intersection, a cross-through. Island-style arrangements can look elegant but are tough to pull off without a lot of furniture, sofa tables, lamps, and plants to make "walls." Like building a fort. You want walls around you for safety. It's human instinct.

Love It!

Living Room "Befores"

Love It!

■ Large and richly colored, this armoire fits the extra-large scale of this house and adds warmth.

■ Deanne's taste clearly leans toward the traditional. The curvy cabriole legs on these tables guided me in choosing complementary pieces. Again, the rich color is a plus in big spaces; the color can help anchor any piece. And when you don't have much furniture, this kind of piece can really help hold an entire grouping together—quite a bit to ask of such a tiny table!

Living Room "Befores"

■ Too much harsh contrast! Everything is all white or all dark, no middle ground or patterns to smooth the transition. No wonder Deanne and Dag were feeling lost!

■ I loved the grandness of the spaces and the bold architecture. The wood floors and plenty of wood trim, and the arched entryway give the open concept good "bones" and warmth.

■ Look at the white sofa. It seemed to drain away what little color there was in the room! I know white and off-white are "safe" choices, but it's clear here how that choice can add up to blah!

The end result: The room is still half-empty, but for now, half of it is furnished "cozy" with a view.

It feels like a real room now and not like a hallway.

How We Did It

■ STEP 1: To create warmth with minimal furnishings, the rug and sofa were moved on the diagonal (that takes up space) near the far wall. A plant, partnered with a floor lamp, softens the niche behind the sofa. A typical arrangement would have the sofa back against the long wall, but that would turn the room into an "event location" without other large-scale furniture to close the conversation cluster.

■ STEP 2: The diagonal placement left the long wall open. The botanical folding screen was the perfect temporary-cum-permanent addition. I love screens for problem-solving: They're a cross between furniture and art and can be moved easily to any room and redecorated time after time.

■ STEP 3: The big surprise was the chair I found in Dag's office—that they didn't want! It was destined to go to the curb; now it has a meaningful home.

■ STEP 4: This is a new home with furniture gradually being gathered. If you don't have seating and are waiting to get more pieces, you may need to make do with an inexpensive accessory piece like this waiting bench. Another favorite problem-solver: Benches fill in gaps, provide seating, and can be redecorated in any fabric and used in any room.

BEFORE

STEP 1

STEP 2

STEP 3

STEP 4

THE CHALLENGE This is a starter home with no particular style, and it's filled with hand-me-down furniture from his mom. **LYNETTE'S SOLUTION** Use dramatic colors to "fill" the visual space. Edit out what you don't like and then fill in with bold accessories.

Daryn, 26, single, has a starter home filled with hand-me-down furniture. Was he enthused about his furnishings? "No, they have all come from my Mom's house. Good quality, but none of it goes together.

Daryn's favorite place? "The living room because I spend most of my time there." Well, I had to discount the comment: It's a sweetheart of a bungalow, but less than 1,000 square feet. The living room is the only room where you can spend any relaxing time. All the other rooms were 10x10 feet or smaller! When I first stepped into the living room, I loved it. Rounded archways lead to adjoining rooms, original "bumpy" plaster still in great shape, and huge windows on two walls. Daryn had already refinished the oak floors and installed some wood wide-slat blinds for privacy. Gorgeous. It's a good house with good bones, but he didn't realize he also had the great beginnings of a high-style interior.

Typically, I would ask him to sort his furniture by photos, but he didn't like any of it! So I sent him to the decorating magazine aisle. I told him to bring me pictures of every room he liked.

When you have awkward proportions in a room, never compromise the conversational distance between seats.

A man of decision, he brought me just one picture! A living room in a Manhattan townhouse with high ceilings, black walls, white traditional moldings, lots of Biedermeier case goods, and all white upholstery! This man has style—but not the $300,000 it would take! And there was no way to transform what he had into a look that specific. So we got to the essence of his attraction to that picture. I quickly realized what he really liked was high contrast and clean lines. He suggested the dark walls. And I was thrilled—besides style, the man has guts. Go for it, Daryn—but let's make it a warm charcoal: It's easier on the eyes, and the cream leather loveseat will look amazing.

So-So...

Leave It.

So-So...

Daryn actually had some good quality pieces. But he didn't recognize their look and lines as having any style. His instinct was working though because he was undecided about these three:

■ The leather loveseat is a classic contemporary. It was my biggest clue to what might work for him.

■ The burgundy chair also had lines, but neither of us liked the color. Amazing how the charcoal walls shifted the color to a dusty, grape-purple. Now it's cool!

■ You can never go wrong with an old classic drop-leaf table. Use it as a dining table or drop one or both leaves and use it as an end table or hall piece.

Leave It.

■ The "grandma" sofa was so named because of its curve and ditsy pattern. But it was a very solid and expensive piece. A slipcover totally transformed it. But please, no drapey throws on the back!

■ These oak tables, like the dining room table, were very solid. Style is still good, but in someone else's house. Not his look at all.

■ Recliners like these are incredibly comfortable. If he had the budget to reupholster, I would've recommended it. But he had enough furniture, and this was his least favorite. So...out, out, out it goes!

How We Did It

■ For under $500 we slipcovered the "grandma sofa" in cream-color synthetic suede (store-bought) and paired it with the existing, stylish cream leather loveseat, moving the burgundy chair into the corner to create a great reading retreat!

■ A crunchy paper floor lamp from IKEA turned a traditional setting into contemporary in one stroke. Wood shades were softened with Pier One tab-top curtains in plain white cotton.

■ We replaced the 1960s oak end tables with a pair of $19 dark mahogany TV tables.

■ Rich, flat latex charcoal paint for the walls adds the needed dramatic contrast. White trim keeps it lively.

■ What made the biggest difference was reorienting the furniture cluster on the diagonal. It removed the rigidity and shifted the proportions of the room. "It's amazing; I love it. My friends are really impressed. I can't believe what it's done to my house! Now I even have a place for my black and white photos." "Black and whites" with oversize white mats and narrow black frames look amazing on dark walls.

BEFORE

BEFORE

My advice for young starters: Keep your look simple, clean, and use color for comfort. Don't buy anything unless you **LOVE** it. Live with less, assemble your collection over time, and be proud of your own personal lifestyle.

THE CHALLENGE They invested in some good quality, neutral-patterned furniture, all in matching suites. Good stuff, but so very bland. **LYNETTE'S SOLUTION** Shake it all up with some furniture "finds" from the back rooms of this historic farmhouse.

Lani and Ted, a young working couple, live in a small 100-year-old house. What's wrong with the furniture? Lani really didn't like it because its oversize scale not only filled the room but felt awkward and lined up against the walls like a furniture warehouse. She'd lost her objectivity, gotten stuck.

Her least-favorite room: "The living room! It's so boring. When we have company, no one likes to sit in there. We always end up in the kitchen or on the porch. I can't stand the furniture!" Wow, now that's a problem. Especially because in this 1900s historic home, moved from its original farm site to the foundation of a dairy barn, the floor plan is farmhouse simple: enter a door from the side porch (now enclosed) into the living room and directly to bedrooms and kitchen. No hallways. If the central room in the house is a downer, the negativity is with you every moment. Got to fix that.

The furniture arrangement was the biggest part of the problem. The solution was to rotate!

The furniture arrangement was the biggest part of the problem. The largest piece, the sofa, crowded the entry, making you feel as though there was no room for you. So you wanted to squeeze by and hurry through to the dining room and kitchen. The chaise was a challenge. And the loveseat parked against the west window blocked the light and view. It was all oriented to the TV, on a stand with an armoire parked next to it. The little electric stove was practical as well as a potential feature but didn't really have a home.

Love It!

So-So...

Love It!

■ Lani and Ted made great choices with their first furniture buys: structurally sound and comfortable. But they realized that all matching pieces can be a big trap, especially in small spaces.

■ The woodstove-style heater might have been a focal point, something around which to arrange the living room, but the scale of the upholstered pieces dwarfed its impact. No deal.

■ Even her favorite picture was oversize! It was important not to place the largest picture above the largest piece of furniture, the sofa. The room would have been unbalanced, and we'd fight to gain visual weight on the other side of the room with accessories.

■ The round maple table was a classic. Had to use it. I removed the glass, gave it a good coat of oil to prevent glass rings, and gave it a place of honor as their new coffee table. While they still aren't crazy about the piece, it will do until they find something unique.

So-So...

■ I tend not to arrange major seating around the TV in the living room; they weren't crazy about that idea, either. When they entertain, the focus is on friends and the conversation. But in a small house, the options are limited. Hide the TV in the armoire and orient seating so it looks conversational but accommodates cozy movie watching.

How We Did It

■ The arrangement, plain and simple! Rotate! Maneuvering the furniture into their rightful positions was very much a Rubik's Cube. Very few options.

■ I started with the realities of TV watching and moved the armoire first. Rather than it being the focal point, now when you enter the living room from the porch you see inviting seating rather than the side of a wood cabinet. The TV was installed in the armoire, eliminating the stand.

■ The chaise became a cozy reading corner. A chaise is a wonderful curiosity. It adds interest to the plainest of sofa/loveseat collections. But remember that it basically sticks out into the room: It's a lounge chair with an ottoman permanently attached, so it can create arrangement problems in a small space. But if you can manage its bulk, a chaise is comfortable, snuggly, and dramatic with an asymmetrical grouping of pictures, lamp, and table.

■ The little traditional piano stool table next to the chaise was hiding under a plant on the enclosed porch.

■ The living room had a great start, but it was cold without the casegoods to add weight. We found the maple coffee table in the corner. Lani didn't feel that the style was appropriate for the upholstered goods. So it was hiding under a display of candles. What she didn't realize is that the upholstery was simple enough that she could combine several unmatched styles.

Open up the furniture arrangement around a primary window. There's something delicious and inviting about being able to walk up to the window to look out rather than being blocked.

BEFORE

BEFORE

When the room is small and the furniture large, keep the wall decor to a minimum.

How We Did It

■ Integrating character pieces like the colonial maple coffee table and end table added the needed warmth. (Other possible options include contemporary glass and metal, classic Euro traditional, and even a chunky rustic table.)

■ Because the room is small and the furniture large, we kept the wall decor to a minimum. Two plates (they're actually candle trays) and a candle sconce fill a large corner behind the sofa, a good example of using "negative" space to fill the eye.

■ We diminished the size of the sofa by cheating it slightly into the dining room entry. That freed up most of the front window for light and view.

■ The loveseat replaced the TV and armoire on the entry wall and angled very slightly to accent a conversational relationship with the sofa.

■ Placing the largest picture and lamps with the largest piece of furniture, the sofa, throws the balance off unless you have equally large objects on the opposite side. Place larger accessories with smaller-scale furniture and vice versa. The coupling is complementary and compensational.

BEFORE

A tiny dated kitchen, but with a baby on the way, there's no time for a full-scale renovation. What now? Make use of the kitchen's classic midcentury style and transform blah into chic, inspired by a favorite print.

Kimberly and Brian, a two-career couple with a pre-school-age child and a baby on the way, live in a ranch house. They say a new updated kitchen is in their plans for the future, but they simply had to do something about the "drabs" now.

I asked Kimberly to tell me about their home. "We love our house. The rooms are large, except for the kitchen. The house has lots of light, especially in the living room. But our kitchen is tiny and I want to paint if I can take the leap to splash color on the walls! We need help."

While the kitchen is definitely on the small side, on closer inspection it had some very good qualities: The cabinets were sturdy. And there was more storage space than meets the eye, typical of an old "stick-built," carpenter-made kitchen. The hardware was solid cast and comfortable to the grip. So my recommendation was to resurface the cabinets. There's nothing wrong with a 1940s or '50s kitchen, with its metal rimmed round corner shelves. Remember what I said earlier about following your heart, decorating for you and not a current style? As it happens, a small picture of a French chef hanging in the kitchen was one of Kimberly's favorites and it had a certain sentimental history. The cues: mustard yellow and black and white checkerboard. If they loved the picture, would they love the combination in real life? They were willing to try.

Follow your heart and decorate for you, not for a current style.

How We Did It

■ We added color and pulled together a look from what was in the room.

■ Old plastic laminate countertops were exchanged for warm wood chopping-block counters. The wood matches the table in the breakfast area, and that helps pull the spaces together.

■ A 2-inch-square checkerboard tile was installed as a backsplash. Since there wasn't a lot of space to cover, the cost for tile was reasonable—but the effect sure was amazing!

■ Kimberly and Brian learned that lighting has everything to do with choosing the right color. The fluorescent fixtures were turning all the yellows to green. Brian tested three different shades of mustard yellow until they found one they loved.

■ New incandescent fixtures were important to generate enough warm light for the room.

The point of attack was to add color and develop a theme based on a loved collectible, adding some punch for drama.

BEFORE

BEFORE

Having just about all of the elements, they were headed in a loose rendition of French country all along, without knowing it. They just needed the reassurance and the OK to go forward.

How We Did It

■ What was interesting is that they already had all of the accessories except for the area rug. They were headed in a loose rendition of French country all along. I recognized the commonalities in their accessories; a style surfaced. I just stuck a label on it. But had they taken a good, hard look at their existing pieces themselves, they probably would have come to the same conclusion—even without the style label. They just needed the reassurance and the OK for the confidence to go forward.

■ They had already committed to replacing the harvest gold appliances with new ovens and a cooktop. That made a big difference on the appliance wall.

■ Refreshing the old cabinets with high-quality white paint brightened the entire room! And next to the yellow soffit and checkerboard backsplash, they really pop. If you've got good cabinetry like this, the smart money is on keeping it.

■ Sometimes, it's the small things that really polish off a room. The existing cabinet hardware was shipped off to an automotive replater to be rebronzed. Better than brand new.

A collection of treasures from travels abroad, mixed in with secondhand finds all together in one room. Organize the room into activity clusters. Find the connections between all the pieces to make better, coordinated groupings.

Shelly and Patrick, in their late thirties, and son Joshua, 17, are an active family with diverse interests living in a tiny bungalow in a historic district.

The thing you like most about your home? "We live in the historic district, so I want to bring out the vintage charm," says Shelly, whose eye for salvaging neighborhood castoffs has resulted in the "Bohemian" collection of great chairs. Here's a home with heart and a couple who believes deeply in surrounding themselves with their lives and not a collection of coordinated furniture.

"I think I may reupholster some of my antique chairs so they all match." I laughed when she said this! Shelly is simply not the matching type. Her two coordinated turquoise chairs were a testament to her fine color sense. Related color instead of matching color is much more interesting. When I first visited their home, I was excited about the mixture of flea market redos and sophisticated pieces. Clearly someone has an eye for shapes and wasn't afraid to mix it up. But I could see the problem. "The house is sunny and

My approach was to reorganize what they already had into groupings that were friendly and intimate.

open though very small." A big plus. What Shelly described as an "open" plan was just that. A large rectangular room with no particular focus. The favorite place wasn't there. And she loved nearly all of her furniture—once she worked on it; she loves to paint and reupholster. She knew she was missing some connectivity and a center. There were four use areas in one small rectangle with no focal point. Easy to get lost. In the end: four favorite places, three separate activity areas, a crayon box of colors, all in one small rectangular room.

Love It!

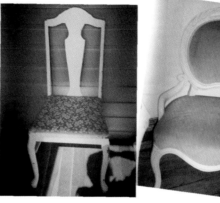

So-So...

Leave It.

Love It!

■ This is the epitome of my message throughout this book. Live with what you love regardless of trends. What a wild collection. I was intrigued. Can we make these work? Where's the connection between them? Every chair had an interesting shape. First clue. Second, she wasn't afraid of color— we can be daring with the upholstery. Some folks call this style "Bohemian."

■ The sofa's seat cushions were in bad shape when she found it. So she made new ones from a coordinating fabric.

■ The leopard stools were her latest curbside find. Just wild enough to make the Bohemian statement.

■ I found the table a little too staid for her. But it could have a life with her semitraditional chair collection.

So-So...

■ These chairs had interesting profiles and the contrasting colors were very sophisticated. I could talk her back into these when I arranged them with the sofa.

Leave It.

■ Stools always come in handy. Send this one to storage until it finds a good home somewhere in the house.

■ This chair is so ugly it's almost a classic! The shiny upholstery is embossed plastic. Very sturdy; someone will re-cover it some day.

■ The TV unit is not so bad. To save money, clean this up and use it.

"It feels like a brand-new house. I'm so excited. And it's all with the things we love."

How We Did It

■ Why leave the walls white? The gallery-white background reinforced the artistry in the individual pieces. Color would have pulled the room in one direction. The looseness is its intrigue.

■ Although there were several ways the primary sofa group could have been arranged, the family seemed to feel comfortable with the sofa against the wall.

■ The sofa now has large-scale companions in the gold club chair and the teal arm show-wood chair both from the "So-So" pile. Now the scale of that side of the room is proportionate and pulled into a comfortable conversation grouping instead of lining the wall.

■ The coffee table found a new home on the opposite side of the room, leaving an opportunity for a pair of Shelly's favorite flea market finds: the 1950s leopard stools, now tables!

■ Shelly and Patrick had three different size rugs from their teaching stint in Pakistan. We moved them so each was appropriate to the size of the furniture grouping: largest with the sofa, smallest with the three chairs in the bay window, and the middle with the third furniture group oriented to the TV. The room suddenly had order.

■ MORE RULE BREAKING: I found the tall dresser—which Shelly had crackled in black and overpainted with rosettes—in the bedroom and moved it to the living room. It's a sweetheart. I followed its rose theme by clustering some of her latest oil paintings above the sofa.

■ Because their bedroom is adjacent to the living area, it had to be redone as well. Now an art-gallery wall and antique-looking linens displaying her throws from Pakistan fill the view.

BEFORE

BEFORE

To start, I shuffled their three rugs, appropriate
to the size of the furniture groupings, to create focal
points. The room suddenly had order.

■ The second grouping is anchored by a bay window, a third around the television, and a fourth by the mirror for band practice.

■ The bay window group was tightened around a coffee table of garden collectibles. Since our first meeting Shelly had reupholstered her white chairs to two shades of turquoise. (I couldn't hold her back!) The green table legs and teals in the chairs are a wonderful nonmatching set that shows off her chair collection and yet maintains connectivity. What was once a "display" of chairs is now another neat place to sit.

■ The bridge between the conversation grouping and the TV grouping is the band's practice area clustered around a keyboard, sax stand, and the gold mirror—a showstopper that was hiding in the bedroom.

■ Every narrow TV unit is going to look about the same, so we cleaned up rather than replace this one. The family prefers individual chairs over a sofa; these also can rotate for band rehearsals. These deck chairs are adjustable for personal comfort.

■ **HOT TIP:** There's a certain honesty to audio-visual equipment. Leave it alone. Don't try to disguise the components with draping plants or knickknacks.

THE CHALLENGE How to remake the kitchen into a happy, inviting place instead of a dark, boring cave–and do it all for under $1,000. **LYNETTE'S SOLUTION** Color! I found my cue for changing the space with the homeowners' collection of cookie jars.

Retired couple Myrna and Ellis love their 1960s ranch house. Bright rooms, good scale—except for a kitchen that's so dark the lights have to be on in midday!

What's their favorite room? "The living room."

And their least favorite? "My kitchen. It's very dark, needs updating, and I simply don't know where to begin!" When it comes to fixing a kitchen, the dilemma is whether to start over ($40,000 and up) or retrofit and make do. "Making do" often has a negative connotation. But with high-tech coatings and terrific options for countertops, flooring, and fixtures, the market offers as many choices for sprucing up as for full-scale remodeling.

The couple had already edited their furnishings when they downsized to this smaller home. They loved what they had and displayed their collections well. But the kitchen didn't fit in. In the living room, new red plaid sofas gave me my cue. Red's a hot decor color, but it's gutsy. They love it.

Working with existing whites is tough. Add a couple of other shades, because a mixture of white and off-white is much more forgiving.

The kitchen was a dark "U" with a single entry. It was like going into a cave: not a happy place to be. The budget was limited so we had to work with the existing countertops, floor, and appliances, all creamy. In this case, because the light source was limited we could have gone in two directions. Leave the cabinets dark and opt for a rich background color: dark and elegant. Or "whiten" the cabinets, cleaning up the colors, and take a hint from Myrna's cookie jar collection. Clearly she prefers bright, clean, crayon colors.

How We Did It

■ We painted the cabinets a soft, creamy white—although a different shade from the countertops and the floor; it both complements and creates a unified background, enhancing what little light is available.

■ The off-white-background wallpaper is scattered with bright floral images, a nod to the homeowners' love of bright colors and a good backdrop for her ceramics.

■ Inspired by Myrna's cookie jar collection, I added some inexpensive ceramics to overdress the wallpapered areas, including the stove backsplash and bulkhead. Ceramic mosaic birdhouses dressed up the window without the obligatory ruffled curtains.

■ Installing a new four-light mini-chandelier not only added atmosphere and much needed light to the room, it's much more attractive than the plain utility fixture that was there.

BEFORE

Use bright, crayon colors to add life to white.

■ Myrna's love of red led me to suggest a wallpaper with red accents, playing off their new red plaid sofas in the adjacent living room.

■ We replaced the vertical blinds with white cotton duck tab-top curtains. If it were a high-traffic area, I would use wood rings; they're easier to slide.

■ The sideboard was a little cluttered with too many items. So we gathered her collection of yellow carnival glass from other rooms to make a more impressive display.

■ **DESIGN LESSON:** If you feel you need to match whites, here's how to come close: Look for the "hidden" color in the white. For example, when you choose a new white, refer to the paint charts many manufacturers offer to present their yellow-, blue-, green-, pink-, or gray-whites.

Everyone's interpretation of true white is different. The same holds true for the so-called white backgrounds in wallpapers. Instead of making yourself crazy looking for a dead-on match, simply stay with the color white that coordinates with what you have. Oddly enough, in the end the slight variations feel natural and not obviously dyed to match.

BEFORE

"Now I think my kitchen is my favorite place! It's so bright. What a change. I love it!"

THE CHALLENGE In this warm and happy home the largest space, the living room, lacked the charm of any of the other rooms. **LYNETTE'S SOLUTION** Color it bright like the other rooms. And bring out the goodies that are hiding upstairs to display and enjoy them.

John and Ruth live with their four teenagers in a lively, two-story home. He's a doctor, she's a talented, well-known quilt artist. "If quilts are your passion, where are they?" I asked Ruth. "A few upstairs, a couple in the kitchen, but most are stored away."

Picking a favorite place was easy—and it showed. "My yellow kitchen; I love yellow. It goes well with my yellowware collection. I also love my bedroom, with an old fruit ladder that holds my quilt collection."

Naming the least-favorite was just as easy. "My living room; I'm tired of the furniture. I need to update the color." Ruth gave me the perfect starting point: "I love antiques and old things. Quilts are my love and passion."

The kitchen is Action Central: bright and full of family mementos, collectibles, and projects. No wonder it's their favorite place. I was drawn

Family history mingled with collectibles and quilts everywhere... until we got to the living room.

to the family table. Fresh pastries warm from the oven, kids' stuff everywhere—like one of her quilts, a patchwork of six on-the-go lives. I wanted to stay. Every other room was the same: I couldn't stop looking around. Family history mingled with collectibles and quilts everywhere until we got to the living room. Two large sofas, a glass coffee table with a showcase top. That was good, but was not them. The color was a drab gray-green. Because the kitchen was yellow, Ruth didn't want to repeat it. The glitch was the flame-stitch upholstery on the sofas in burgundy/navy/mauve/wine. This was tough. And it was the darkest room in the house. We had to stay away from cool colors, yet the warmer tones were in the kitchen and front hall.

Love It!

So-So...

Leave It.

Love It!

■ Formal, investment pieces along with a few favorite "finds," like her sewing cabinet and green painted cupboard in the dining room.

■ For a large, active family, having two full-size sofas was a smart decision, and the dark upholstery was a practical choice. So Ruth was doing the right things. But choosing a color for an already shaded room based on the burgundy/navy flame-stitch sofas and gray carpet pushed her into drab tones. That was the trap.

So-So...

■ Ruth's choices of these surprised me. I'd have thought she would love these pieces. But she was bored with them. "Not enough character" was how she felt about them.

Leave It.

■ Send these pieces to my house! I love distressed cabinets.

■ These are called "primitives." They give a room texture, whimsy, and intrigue—and they always prompt a speculative conversation that starts with "Where were these in a previous life?"

The solution: Follow the lead of this lively kitchen to recolor the living room walls. And bring on the "stuff." Let's get some personality into this room.

How We Did It

The living room looked as if it was in someone else's house. There was little or no evidence of the lively personality I saw elsewhere in the home. Recolor the walls to bring in the liveliness of the kitchen. And bring on the "stuff." Let's get some personality into this room.

■ We were looking for brilliance. Turquoise has the properties of yellows. Bright, uplifting, clean, and happy. She loved it.

■ As we approached the photo shoot day, Ruth went "junking" and found a green frame from an old room screen. We needed an anchor to pull the eclecticism from the other rooms into the living area. This was it. Collectibles are tough to display without either a series of frames or shelves. Hang the frame by itself on the wall above the sofa as a corral for lots of small items. What fun we had as the kids came

"I love my new colors. What a huge difference it made adding the buttery yellow accents to the clear blue."

Don't stash the things you love in closets. Put them out where you can see and enjoy them every day.

BEFORE

home from school and made suggestions for the contents. It became a whole-house treasure hunt.

■ One of the items in Ruth's "Leave It" pile was a tall distressed cabinet that stood on the second floor landing storing a daughter's stuffed animals. It was perfect for the new living room. It loosened up the staid furniture and has become the anchor to the new look.

■ In the end, most of the main furniture pieces stayed—and stayed in place! Now these pieces are surrounded by the things that Ruth and

her family love. Every day the family is greeted by these items as they move through the house.

■ Because the family's style flows through all the rooms—as does the color scheme—things can move when they want a change. A different quilt can be put on display in the living room, for example. Even the display inside the coffee table can be changed to freshen the displays of their memories from time to time.

BEFORE

THE CHALLENGE While they love their bungalow, they don't think their furniture fits with a family-style look. **LYNETTE'S SOLUTION** Sort their furniture to define their "Love It" pieces, and work on connecting them to the house. It's all actually very compatible!

Shayn and Aaron, a two-career couple, live in a historic Craftsman bungalow with their twin preschool-age children.

They love certain furniture pieces for comfort, but don't like where the pieces are; the look isn't doing anything for the happy, family-style atmosphere they want. "We've lived here for six years and simply cannot figure out how to paint or decorate! Help!"

I asked for their favorite place in the house. "The living room, because it has lots of light, is very open." The wide bungalow has a rectangular living room reaching from side to side across the front, backed by a dining area/hallway leading through the kitchen to the rear of the house. Two bedrooms are on the side, and a possible master bedroom in the attic can be accessed by a pull-down utility staircase. This is going to be a big job!

I found the house had an attitude. Wonderful windows and well-loved oak floors. This house has guts and we need to bring that out.

Shayn and Aaron are so anxious and frustrated that it didn't take much to launch them into a full renovation—all in time to make our photography deadline!

But first, THE PLAN: When I asked about favorite furniture, it brought out a much different reaction. What they thought they liked on the first sorting of photos, in fact, wasn't where they ended up. This happens. It starts with "Yes, I like the leather sofas, and yes, they're comfortable." But later it becomes "Well, I thought I liked them in the living room, but they're taupe and that's not our favorite color. In fact, they'd look really good in the lower-level den."

Love It!

So-So...

Leave It.

Love It!

■ Shayn and Aaron loved their furniture for the right reasons: comfort, color, intrigue, and memories. But their vision for their home went in an entirely different direction.

■ Where do you make the big change? My advice is to think about your investment. They knew the house was for keeps and eventually the leather furniture would find a home when they remodeled for a den/family room on the lower level.

■ All their other loves were very workable within the character of their historic bungalow home.

So-So...

■ The leather chairs found their way to the basement with the sofas.

■ The built-in buffet in the dining room turned out to be a gem. We replaced the sliding glass doors with proper cabinet doors and vintage hardware, then painted it white. It's a whole new piece.

Leave It.

■ The coffee table wasn't that bad. For now, it's usable and in the character of the new furniture.

■ I wasn't able to talk them into keeping two blue colonial chairs. They're comfortable—a little loose-jointed but bold. Not one to pass up a good castoff, they're being reupholstered and refinished for my own den at the ranch!

How We Did It

■ We essentially ignored the three stacks of photos and concentrated on colors. Brights were out, naturals were in, but the actual colors would depend on the replacement sofas.

■ Budget-conscious and living in a small town with only two furniture stores, they worked to find multicolor plaids—two of them! One a smaller scale and predominantly coral red, and the other, a larger scale print in brick and sage. That was the cue we were looking for.

■ I found the house had an attitude. It had this handcrafted evidence in the woodwork, wide Western-style windows, and well-loved and patched oak floors. This house had guts and we needed to bring that out. Love and lots of sweat equity prompted a two-career couple with 4-year-old twins to pull out the stops.

■ Within days of my first visit, and to my complete surprise, they poked a hole in the dining room ceiling, began construction of a staircase, disassembled all of the old double-hung windows, and stripped generations of paint, ripped up the carpet, and refinished the floors!

■ The idea was to work with what they had...and they did exactly that. Even the old blond cabinet with the rippled glass sliding doors that was tucked into the dining room alcove was refurbished with new hinged doors, painted, and replaced to serve as a buffet. I was stunned. They now had a vision, and that's all it took after six years of struggling.

They now had a vision, and that's all it took after six years of struggling.

BEFORE

The heavy-patterned sofas are practical for the kids, yet grown-up enough for this young couple to entertain, and offer a nice contrast to the new wall color.

How We Did It

■ I didn't want the house to feel like it was decorated "yesterday." We needed to complete the charm. So I suggested a 6-inch board rail around the perimeter of the room that would split the color on the wall, sage below and pale squash above. Aaron was worried about the gold, but he loves it now. Conservative, but lively at the same time.

■ The dining room functions as the primary traffic lane and, as well, the main play space for the boys. So an area rug would be impractical to use.

■ Instead of being tucked under the staircase, Shayn's desk (and the kids' computer spot) found its way into a bright living room corner, now one of her favorite places. The heavy-patterned sofas are practical for the kids, yet grown-up enough for this young couple to entertain.

■ We even resurrected a glass coffee table that was on its way out, for the new living area.

BEFORE

BEFORE

Shayn's comment to her husband: "Oh my gosh, what a difference. Now we need to start the kitchen, honey!" I say, Go for it!

THE CHALLENGE A beautiful home full of beautiful furnishings and distinctive collectibles, but these homeowners had lost their enthusiasm. **LYNETTE'S SOLUTION** A whole house, room-by-room scramble: a big rearrange-to-rediscover the romance project.

Natalie and Dan, a professional couple, recently became empty nesters. Now it's time for their French country style home to make a change too.

Natalie's plea: "Please help me with the master bedroom. I am attempting *again* to introduce color, texture, and change. The master bedroom is my sanctuary." So there I was standing in the middle of an enormous bedroom, so large it miniaturized a king-size bed. Two walk-in closets at the far, far corners. Adjacent workout room the size of most living rooms and an en suite spa—it looked as though they moved in yesterday and parked the furniture. Taming the bedroom became the key objective. Determined to work with what they already had, I began my hunt to find pieces to fill the space and break up the 6-piece matching bedroom suite. That's where the adventure started.

My search for furniture for the bedroom led me to the most beautiful room in the house: It occupies the front corner of the floor plan,

Color was important but not until we got the ambient space under control.

double-high ceilings, two arched windows cornering the most precious view of the mountains, granite fireplace, and French doors leading from the foyer. The only things in the room: a Victrola, a wing chair, a round antique table and a grand piano. "Who plays the piano?" I asked, assuming a concert master in the house who's passion merited the best room. "My daughter," she responded, "who has moved away to college, and rarely plays." In my wanderings and casual conversation I discovered they had no dining room. It soon became clear that this project was expanding into a whole-house project.

The Family Room "Before" the Scramble

"Before the Scramble"
The Family Room

■ Talk about "fruit basket upset"! This house was chock-full of great stuff—but so much of it in the wrong spaces.

■ The grand piano, though hardly used, had the best spot in the house. The piano ate up every inch—there was hardly room for any other furniture. But look at the light flowing into this room: What potential!

The Living Room/Kitchen Area "Before" the Scramble

Living Room/Kitchen Area

■ Big, bold leather seating pieces dominated the living room. And it's a big space, so it could handle the heavy look. The space, however, lacked warmth. All that great furniture but it was cold looking.

■ Great kitchen! Inviting, functional, etc. But see that tiny eating area over by the windows? That's the only "dining room" this house had!

Master Bedroom

■ You couldn't ask for a more grand space for a bedroom. But it was so big I could see instantly that it had to be divided into more comfortable, useable spaces.

The Master Bedroom "Before" the Scramble

■ The far end had interesting shapes, and the closet doors on diagonal walls added interest. But those elements looked almost out of place compared to the grand openness of the opposite side of the room.

What I discovered was the absence of a dining room. Their dining area was in fact a breakfast area tucked in the rear of the kitchen. When I asked what I was missing, Natalie confessed that was indeed an issue...the next project. But where?

How We Did It

High ceilings and huge views—the perfect space for a dramatic dining area day or night. But we had to find room for the baby grand.

■ To cut the width of the room, we first positioned the table on the diagonal. Much more interesting and underlined the fireplace as a feature instead of a backdrop.

■ The piano swapped places with the giant Don Quixote sculpture which reaches into the double-height ceiling.

■ We lifted the impression of the tall walls by accessorizing the china cabinet with a large urn.

■ Natalie's carpeted music room now dining area got oversize tiles with granite insets.

■ She can add an area rug at some time, but it will have to be large enough so that the chairs don't catch on the edges when they're scooted back.

■ Her collection of pottery was given a place of honor on the mantel and the overscale picture was replaced with the horizontal pears picture, all creating a lowered composition that reinforced the width of the fireplace and, subsequently, the wall.

BEFORE

BEFORE

Work through the "get to know your home" exercises and you'll rediscover the romance. You're likely to find unexpected pleasures in what you already have.

How We Did It

Natalie's living room was well furnished. But it felt a little chunky and cold. We needed to create tighter, more inviting relationships between the furniture pieces and the accessories.

■ We first tightened the leather furniture pieces, pulling them closer together, more conversational.

■ The piano warmed the corner where the Don Quixote sculpture used to live. The piano's generous size beautifully fills the space, right up to the edge of the conversation grouping.

■ The sofa is very imposing. It needed to be backed and flanked by more traditional pieces to warm it up. So we found a sofa table for its back and moved Dan's favorite, the round marble-top foyer table, to its side. The solid look and feel of the table is a good match for the sofa.

■ The handpainted console enlivened the wall at the far end of the sofa and made the perfect base for an inviting vignette. When you approach the room from the front door, that corner is the first space you see. So the detailed sailboat model got that prime real estate!

BEFORE

BEFORE

BEFORE

How We Did It

■ Back to the original challenge: Divide and conquer! Then add color. Natalie found a pair of round-cornered end cabinets with exquisite inlay. She sent me a Polaroid with a note: "Will they work?" They're unique and beautiful; we'll make them work. A carpenter built a bridge unit with a television on one side and full-length mirrors on the back to create the much-needed dressing salon. At 7 feet tall, the piece cuts the vaulted ceiling down to size.

■ I took the damask bench from the spa bathroom and put it at the end of the bed.

■ Bedding was our first try at color. Bold was the only answer. A traditional tapestry bed set in the deepest wines and reds. Topping the headboard with a pair of over-framed abstracts kept the eclecticism going and conquered the triangular bed wall. We broke up the matchy-matchy night tables by exchanging one for a small dresser. At least the scale was different. One day she'll color the room and possibly add drapes. But my job is done. Natalie and Dan got the picture, and I'm sure they'll continue to enjoy the hunt for exciting additions.

What Happened Here?

Natalie, as talented as she is with her decorating projects and good taste, had momentarily lost her objectivity. It's so very normal to not be able to see your home and your things any more.

It doesn't take much to reopen one's eyes and become excited again with your lifelong collection. The catalyst is the analysis I spoke of earlier. Work through the "Get to know your home" exercises and you'll rediscover the romance.

The nemesis bedroom was intimidating, overpowering and boring. It needed to be reduced in size physically and emotionally! A room divider was the answer.

Now that you've seen how these homeowners did it, you can too! Creating the home you want is easy if you know yourself. Be brutally honest about your furniture and your lifestyle. Then act with No Compromises!

CREDITS

Our thanks to the following companies for providing
many of the products used in the makeovers
featured on pages 136-213
■ California Cut Flower Association
■ Designer's Fountain Lighting
■ Glidden Paint
■ Home Decorators Collection
■ IKEA
■ Pier One Imports
■ Sherwin-Williams Wallpaper

Provence
Roman Colosseum (Bull fight)
  Roman architecture in the world.

18th century fabrics — Den'ime

Castelas — — olive grove.

Mirabeau (Fountains)
  City of Exon — Marious street
  archway
          columns
  Exon — Home of Paul Cézan